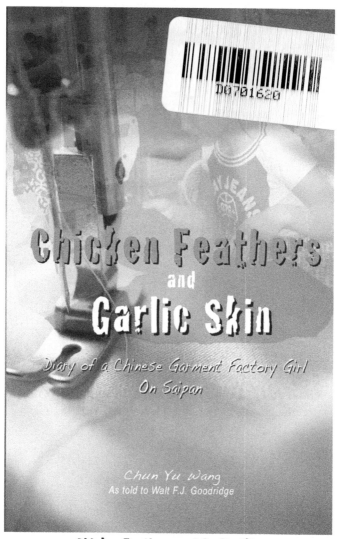

Chicken Feathers and Garlic Skin
鸡毛蒜皮
Diary of a Chinese Garment Factory Girl
On Saipan

CHUN YU WANG
As told to Walt F.J. Goodridge

Chicken Feathers and Garlic Skin

Diary of Chinese Garment Factory Girl on Saipan

© Chun Yu Wang & Walt F.J. Goodridge. All rights reserved.

Published by Walt F.J. Goodridge
dba a company called W

*Books, apps, audio, video, merchandise,
courses, Walt's passion projects, freebies
and more from a company called W!*
www.waltgoodridge.com/store

Distributed by The Passion Profit Company
Educational institutions, government agencies, libraries
and corporations are invited to inquire about quantity discounts.
Contact: sales@passionprofit.com; (646) 481-4238

Retail Cost: $14.95
ISBN-10: 0-9745313-4-0 **ISBN-13:** 978-0-9745313-4-2
Library of Congress Cataloging-in-Publication Data
Wang, Chun Yu, 1974-
Chicken feathers and garlic skin : diary of a Chinese garment factory
girl / Chun Yu Wang.
p. cm.
Includes bibliographical references and index.
ISBN 978-0-9745313-4-2 (alk. paper)
1. Wang, Chun Yu, 1974- 2. Women clothing workers--China--
Biography. 3. Clothing trade--Saipan. I. Title.
HD6073.C62C693 2009
331.6'2511360967--dc22
[B]
2009000312

Paperback printed in the United States of America Second Edition

Acknowledgments

I wish to thank:

Yu Wei Hong (余偉紅) aka "Tiger Hong," Liu Da Mei (劉大梅),
Zhang Gui Rong (張桂榮), Guo Qiong Ying (郭□ 英), Liu Qing
Ling (刘□ 林), Aunt Zhu (朱阿姨)

My parents, Wang Heng Jun (王恒俊) and Gu Xue Ying (顾学英)
who gave me life, and made me everything that I am. I wish you
both health and happiness.

Robert Jones, of Triple J, who helped me at a difficult time. I never
got a chance to really thank him face to face as he's always so busy.
So I will use this opportunity to do so. Thank you, and I hope your
business becomes more and more prosperous.

Everyone in my family who helped me, and everybody who is
mentioned in this book. Because of you, and through all the joys as
well as the trials and hardships, I now have a story to tell.

Dedication

To my family

Table of Contents

Translating and transcribing *Chicken Feathers and Garlic Skin* with Chun Yu Wang was a unique, enlightening and educational experience. As editor, my role has been merely that of scribe. Chun Yu wrote her manuscript and notes herself, by hand, in traditional Mandarin characters. She then used an electronic translator to find the closest approximation to certain idioms and concepts unique to Mandarin. The transcription process consisted of the two of us sitting at a table—she reading from her notes, and translating it herself—narrating to me in English.

Her relatively recent introduction to the English language made the process a little slower. However, even though her command of English is still developing, I didn't want to have a human translator get in the way of the authenticity of her work, or affect her own developing writing style.

Based on what I've learned about Chinese language and culture in the process, I felt it was important to allow Chun's communication style to exist in an untainted form as it gives us some insight into her unique world view, cultural perspective, and perhaps even a culturally-informed, and gender-specific approach to life that may itself be part of the story. In addition I wanted to remain true to what I feel is the inherent poetry, the embedded proverbs and peculiarities of Mandarin speech. There's a rhythm to the language, a tempo in the phrasing, and efficiency in the syntax that often gets lost in translation.

As we proceeded, I realized that some of the words the electronic translator offers as English equivalents are a bit archaic, or very rarely used in everyday conversation. This was quite amusing at times, and we had fun with the machine's choice of words in its translations of Chinese idioms.

Thus, for example, a factory monitor is described as an [insatiably avaricious], woman who [covets small advantages, and hankers after petty gains]—a turn of phrase few modern western writers might choose for themselves, but is highly appropriate for communicating the shades and subtlety of concepts in Mandarin which might not have a direct English equivalent. Some of these I kept. Others I replaced with more common, everyday language.

This decision to use her own developing language skills to translate from Mandarin to English results in a simply told, yet profound story unencumbered by the intricacies of multi-syllabic and layered English words and idioms. It lends itself to something

I've learned personally while living abroad. When two people communicate from across a cultural and language divide, there is a mutual effort to meet each other someplace in the middle.

As the reader of her book, your efforts to meet Chun Yu halfway are just as necessary as her efforts to communicate her thoughts to you. The simplicity of communication style is both endearing and part of her charm. It represents who she is at this moment as a Chinese garment factory worker on Saipan, and thus, is as much a part of her story as any of the characters and events she chronicles. The read becomes as much of the experience as the telling of the experience itself. You are challenged, therefore, to find a middle ground of understanding and commonality.

But don't mistake this simplicity for passivity. As you'll discover, Chun Yu was the quiet rebel behind three different labor disputes on Saipan. She has within her, by virtue of being born in the Year of the Tiger, a natural fighting instinct spurred by a desire for justice. Her story is also compelling for other reasons.

Keep in mind, that as a Chinese garment factory worker on Saipan, life is a bit different than for you and me. When you read of the experiences of these factory girls, it is important to recognize those cultural differences. For those readers who are living in non-communist, western-influenced societies you may take certain things for granted which may need to be explained for you to fully appreciate the subtleties and nuances of the story being told.

For example, because of the typical level of income, as well as Chinese immigration policies, many factory girls have never flown on an airplane, or even been outside of China. Because of gender roles, and the Chinese population's traditional relationship to authority, many are reluctant to make waves or question rules. Because of the high value placed on saving face, many are not willing to risk embarrassment on foreign soil—the details of which may get back to shame their families in China. Because of the relationship between men and women, or between fathers and daughters, many have never made decisions for themselves. Because of the nature of government control, many are not aware of their "rights" separate from government dictates (a foreign concept), and hence do not exercise such rights abroad for fear of retribution. And finally, because of the control many of the factories themselves wish to exert over the girls, many are discouraged from even learning the English language while employed.

When such realities frame your cultural context, historical background, and thus your world view, how do you communicate your thoughts, fight for your rights, or search for happiness in a strange land beyond the walls of a factory compound? Such is the plight of the typical factory girl.

Yet, here it is: her story, in her words, transcribed with as little of my influence as possible. My task was to listen to her thoughts and what she wished to communicate, transcribe them, tone intact, into grammatically correct English sentences, intervening only to ask her questions to fill in certain gaps, clarify any apparent inconsistencies in the storytelling, or explain certain concepts which may be foreign to non-Chinese readers.

Chun Yu, the author, has a natural storyteller's love of words, along with a memory for details that made *Chicken Feathers and Garlic Skin* as much of an enjoyable experience co-authoring, as I trust you shall have in reading it. I hope that you will cherish the experience of getting to know her through her story.

Walt F.J. Goodridge
Co-Author/Editor

p.s. About the Title

My originally-conceived title for this book was simply *Factory Girl*. It's still a title I like, but, once I heard the Chinese idiom "chicken feathers and garlic skin" during a transcription session with Chun, I knew we had to use it.

"Chicken feathers and garlic skin" is the rubbish left when cooking a chicken. Being worthless, they attract little attention. The phrase is used to describe "petty things; things of no importance; things often overlooked as having no merit or value." It is perhaps the perfect metaphor for the often faceless, nameless girls who toil away in the garment factories of the world sewing designer clothing for consumers around the world; girls who often go overlooked in the public dialogue and perception of the world at large.

As you'll discover, everyday Chinese language, is rich with other such idioms and proverbs (italicized within the text), which have been used as titles for several of the chapters and sections.

Chapter 1:
Wolves Ahead
and Tigers Behind ▲

Tigers...

"If you don't give me an answer right now," I said threateningly to my ex-boyfriend, "I will marry him! I mean it!"

It was November of 1996. I was 22 years old. I had broken up with my boyfriend two months before, but it was hard to forget about him. So, I met him for lunch that day in November, to tell him about the new man who had just proposed to me. I asked him what he thought about it. He didn't answer me.

A few months earlier, on a sunny morning in September, someone had introduced me to the man who would become my husband. That same evening he took me to meet his mother. One month later, he asked me to marry him. I told him I would have to ask my mother and father first.

My mother and father both went to his house to meet him. They didn't give any input about what they thought about him. They only told me that if I wanted to marry him, it would be all right with them. It wasn't until years later that my older brother told me that they hadn't liked his character, but they didn't want to be responsible if things didn't work out well between us. So, now, with this new man's proposal as an option, I gave my ex-boyfriend a final chance.

"If you don't give me an answer right now," I now threatened my ex-boyfriend, "I will get married to him."

When he still didn't answer—in his usual indecisive way—I got angry. I got married to my husband—a man I had only known for two months—a few weeks later in December of 1996.

My new husband once told me he knew that if he had waited more than a month to marry me, that I wouldn't be his wife. He was probably right. I only married him out of anger.

A month after we got married, we had a big fight. It was over the silliest of things. My husband's brother had come over to visit to play video games. Before his brother even finished playing one of the games, my husband decided that *he* wanted to play. I thought he was being childish and selfish.

"You *always* play that game," I said. "Your brother is only here for a few hours, let *him* play it instead."

But my husband didn't listen. I took the game card from the table and walked away with it into the bedroom. I hid the card so he wouldn't be able to play.

He went to the bedroom and searched for a long time, but when he couldn't find it, he got angry. The way he carried on scared me. He threw things—clothes, books, etc. He broke things. I got mad, too. I got the card and threw it at him.

"Here's your card!" I shouted.

Even his own brother said he was out of order, and acting out of control.

"She was only joking," his brother told him. "Why are you acting so crazy?"

When I saw this, I wanted to leave and go to my mother's house. I started packing my suitcase. When his brother saw what was happening, he called their mother.

"I want a divorce," I cried to her over the phone.

"Okay, so go!" my husband shouted from the other room.

His brother blocked the door preventing me from leaving.

His parents were there in less than ten minutes. His brother told them what happened. When they heard, even his parents got angry with him. They scolded him and told him to clean up the apartment. He refused stubbornly, and they argued.

I was determined to leave, but his parents begged me not to. They knelt and pleaded with me. It had been only a month, they told me. They wanted me to give it more time for things to get better.

My husband's family was not rich. He was also five years older than I was. He was 28 at the time. That's old in China. He also wasn't very communicative or outgoing, and tended to stay home a lot. His parents knew that if I left him—with his personality and habits—it would be difficult for their son to find another bride.

"Let her go!" he shouted again to them, stubbornly.

I got even angrier. The arguing in the house got louder.

With all the shouting and noise, some of our neighbors came to the house to see what all the commotion was about. Nobody could control him or me. We were both too angry.

Meanwhile, my father-in-law knew that my husband had a good friend whom he respected and to whom he would listen. My father-in-law decided to call him to come over to help the situation.

My husband's friend arrived soon after, and after they talked for about ten minutes, my husband came to me to apologize. However, for me, it was too late. I knew that I wanted a divorce.

"No," I said.

He then cleaned up the apartment, then got on his knees and begged me to stay. I stayed, but I knew then I did not love him.

That night, his parents went to buy food for us to have a conciliatory dinner at our house.

My husband and I stayed together, unhappily, for the next four years. Things have not improved. We don't have a common language. We think differently. When we talk about things, we do not agree. We find no common ground. He thinks only about the moment. He doesn't think about the future. He's always thinking about things getting worse, never better. We're just incompatible.

When we fought, things would often get very bad. We wouldn't talk. We would ignore each other for days at a time, and sleep in different beds. It was a very cold relationship.

"Why do I need a husband?" I once asked him. "I can do everything myself. You cannot make money. You cannot improve our life. You have me do all the work."

The truth is, I've never told my mother and father how bad things were. If I did, they would probably just remind me that it had been my own choice to marry him.

I've tried many times to leave, but there was always pressure from his parents as well as my parents. A divorce would bring embarrassment to our families. Yet staying is unbearable.

To stay or to leave? In China, we have a saying: *wolves ahead and tigers behind,* to describe a situation where every option brings danger and uncertainty. Such are the tigers behind me.

Me...

My name is Wang, Chun Yu. *Wang* is my family name. *Chun Yu* is my given name. In China, we say our family name first, and our given name second. I am from China, Wu Xi. In China, we say our country's name first, and our city name second. I was born in 1974, the year of the Tiger.

My parents are both over sixty years old. They have two children. My brother is five years older than me. My father worked in a factory for thirty years as the boss. My mother was a housewife.

My parents are very kind and affable, understanding and reasonable. They have good hearts and are very considerate. They are very honest. They taught me how to respect others, and to take pleasure in helping people. They taught me how to endure hardships. I love my parents. They also love me.

I grew up in the country. When I was seventeen years old, I went to the city to work in a garment factory. We got paid once a year. I know it is hard to imagine. In China, you can work for an entire year before you get your first paycheck. A factory boss in China can do that if he is a private owner. The government didn't own the factory I worked in.

I worked every day, with no holidays to rest. I had overtime every day. Every year, I saved money to give to my parents so that when I got married they could pay a dowry.

My husband worked at a car factory. Every month, he made a small amount of money—never enough to pay for power, water, telephone and rent. He, too, got paid once a year.

...and the Wolves

"Aunt" Zhu was the first person who told me about Saipan. It was in 1999. At that time, Aunt Zhu was about 55 years old. She was a retired seamstress, and my boss in China hired her to work in our factory to teach us sewing techniques. We called her "aunt" because of the special relationship she developed with us. She's a very kind and caring person.

"Do you want to go to another country to work?" she asked me one day. "You are young. You should go to another country to make some money—more money than you can make in China."

"No, I don't want to," I said.

A few days later, she asked me again. She also called me and asked. This time she told me that the country was called Saipan. She had never been there, but she had friends who worked there.

"Where exactly is Saipan?" I asked her. "I think I've heard about this place, but I can't remember who told me."

"Saipan is part of America," she said, "but it is very far from the US. It's a small island, but it has good salaries—higher than in China—and they have beautiful oceans, too. If you work there for three years, you can earn much more money than here."

I had never thought about going to another country to work, but when she told me more about Saipan, my heart became noisy and restless. I thought about what she said. Imagine! In three years, I could make almost $30,000 US dollars—that was about ¥240,000* [yuan]. That would be very good for me. It might take me ten or twenty years to make that much money in China.

From that time, I started to imagine what Saipan might be like, and how magical a place it might be. I started dreaming of going. Maybe life was offering me a special opportunity.

When I told my mother and father that I wanted to go to Saipan, they weren't very happy. Their first reason was that my son was very young. He was only three years old at the time.

They also said they had only one female child—me. They wanted me to take care of them as they were getting old.

The third reason was if I left them, they would feel deep anxiety and would always think about me. They would miss me.

Also, if my husband was left by himself, they told me, he, a man would not be able to take care of a baby. Men don't know how to take care of babies.

They were also afraid that with a lot of money in my possession that I might be a victim of some sort of fraud or scam. It happens a lot in China. Truthfully, I was afraid of that, too.

But, I didn't care that my family wasn't happy about me going overseas. I always act according to my own will, and I was intent on having my way. Nobody could stop me. Nobody could decide for me. Nobody could change my mind. I was now determined to go to Saipan.

The exchange rate at this time was approximately: $1US = ¥8 (Yuan).

They say that every family has a skeleton in the closet. Mine was that my relationship with my husband was not good.

In China, we say *out of thirty-six plans, the best is to get away at once.* Even though I did not know what the future in Saipan would be like—the unknown wolves ahead—I *did* know that I was very unhappy with my life in China. This made me want to leave even more to escape the tigers behind.

When I told my husband I wanted to go to Saipan, he, too, objected. He said our son was too young, and furthermore, we didn't have the money to pay the fee to the employment agency.

I told him that I could borrow the money, but he didn't listen. We argued back and forth every single day for two weeks. He had many reasons why I should not go. He said because I was always sick—with colds and stomach pain—that even if I made money on Saipan, most of it would go for medicine. My husband has no desire for progress. He's timid and fearful about everything.

One thing that my parents, my husband and I all agreed upon, however, was the fate of my son. I worried what his life would be like if I were to leave. So, I went to see my husband's father. I told him that in three years, when I came back, I would buy a house for us, and life would be better than it was at the time. I asked him to take care of my son while I was away, and he agreed. From the beginning, he supported my decision to go to Saipan. My husband's father is a more sensible and broad-minded man.

Eventually, my husband agreed and said I could go. I contacted the agency, and a few days later, I got the message to go to take a qualifying test. Before I could go to Saipan, I learned, I had to take a test to prove I could sew well enough.

My Best Friend, Da Mei

My best friend is Liu Da Mei. Da Mei is married and has a son. She and I worked together. She's from China, Chang Zhou.

Da Mei's husband was always in another city working, so most of the time, they weren't together. She was also not a rich person. I wanted Da Mei with me in Saipan so I would have a friend, and not feel so uncomfortable and alone. I asked her if she wanted to go with me. She, too, had never heard of Saipan.

When I told her what I knew about Saipan, she got as excited as I was about the idea.

In October, 1999, we went to Nan Tong to take the qualifying test for a company doing business on Saipan. Nan Tong was a two-hour bus ride from Wu Xi.

It was about 6:30 a.m. on a rainy day. Da Mei and I and a man named Mr. Wong took the bus to Nan Tong. Mr. Wong was a friend of Aunt Zhu. He knew the director at one of the factories on Saipan. If we were hired, Mr. Wong would get part of the fee we paid to the agency.

Once we got to Nan Tong, we took a taxi to the office where the test was being given.

If we passed the test, the company manager would let us know the results right away, and interview us on the spot. The atmosphere in the test room was very serious. We got nervous.

Fortunately, even though we were nervous, Da Mei and I passed the qualifying test!

In the interview that followed, the manager asked many questions. *Are you married? Do you have children? Why do you want to go to Saipan? How many years do you want to work in Saipan? How much money do you want to make?*

Mr. Wong had told us we had to answer every question correctly, or else they would delete our names from the list. For example, if the boss asked why you wanted to go to Saipan, some girls might say, "I want to visit another country to see what it's like." That's not the right answer. You should say, "I want to make more money to make my life better."

If they asked you how long you wanted to stay, they didn't want you to stay too short, or too long. If you said "one year" that was no good. After one year, you would just be learning to do the job, and would provide only a few months of productivity for the factory in Saipan. If you said you wanted to work more than three years, that was no good, either, because if you stayed too long, you deprived other people of contracts, and the company in China couldn't make money. The right answer was "three years."

When the boss started asking me those questions, I got very nervous. I was scared that if I said something wrong, I would be disqualified and sent home.

"Where are you from?" he first asked me.

"Wu Xi," I said.

"Who introduced you to us?"

"Mr. Wong," I said. "He's also from Wu Xi."

I was lucky he only asked me a few questions. I passed the interview! I was very happy. I cannot describe how happy I was.

Da Mei passed her interview too!

When we heard that we passed, Da Mei and I hugged each other with happiness right there in the office. We were jumping excitedly, and crying. Not everybody had the chance and the luck that we did. Some people had to take the test three or four times to pass. Others passed the test, but said the wrong thing in the interview and were sent home.

I heard somebody say that because the factory director in Saipan was from Wu Xi, that they gave us special consideration. We found out that the test grader was also from Wu Xi. I don't know if that is true, but I am glad I passed.

The agency told us what kind of materials and documentation we needed, and how much money we would have to pay. We went back to Wu Xi elated, but also a bit nervous.

On our way home, we decided we would play a joke on everyone by acting as if we had failed. When we arrived home and saw my husband and his parents, we told them we didn't pass the test. We acted very sad.

"We knew you wouldn't pass the test," they said. Too bad."

But Da Mei and I could not control ourselves any more. We couldn't hold back any longer, and started laughing. Then they realized we were joking and that we had actually passed!

But even though we passed the test and the interview, we still had not paid the recruitment fee yet, and Da Mei was not sure she would be able to find the money.

The total fee that we had to pay the agency was ¥28,000, or about $3,500US. The first half of the fee was $1,750US. They gave us one week to find the first half. That was more than I had saved.

That night, I called my uncle—my father's sister's husband —told him what I wanted to do, and asked to borrow ¥3,200, about $400US.

He didn't want to lend me the money. He said my father needed to be the one to open his mouth to request the loan. He was afraid that if I lost the money, that I would not be able to pay him back. So my father had to be the one to borrow it. If someone stole the money, or if I could not pay it back, he thought, he would be able to ask my father—not me—to pay it back.

Nobody can imagine how I felt. In China, we have a saying that translates most directly as *through a door crack, people can only see a small view of a person*. My uncle was looking at me as a poor young girl with no means to pay him back—through just the little crack that provided the image he had of me. He didn't see my future, who I could become, or the money I would make.

In China we say, *though one is poor he still has lofty aspirations.* I never asked my uncle again for anything, and I never called him again since that day. *One day I will get richer than you*, I promised myself.

I borrowed ¥16,800 ($2,100US) from my husband's father. When he gave it to me he said, "This money is very important. It's for your husband's mother's diabetes medicine."

I told him I knew how important it was, and promised him that I would give it back no matter what. In China, it's very hard to save money, so I know it was a lot of money to them. If I didn't give it back, it would affect their lives very much.

Lastly, I borrowed from my brother. When I asked him, my brother did not say anything. He simply gave me the money— ¥3,200 ($400US)—the next day. With the ¥8,000 I had already saved, I now had the money I needed.

A few days later, I went by bus to Jang Yin city to take a physical exam and get the necessary medical approval. Everything went well. With the medical approval, I had everything I needed. Da Mei's situation, however, was not as good.

Da Mei's husband still didn't know that she wanted to go to Saipan. She hadn't told him. When she found out that she needed to take a physical, and that she needed money to pay the fee, it was only then that she found the courage to tell him.

Da Mei's life was not any better than mine. She, too, asked friends and family for help, but they couldn't lend her any money. She also asked me, but I couldn't help her either. Da Mei was very distraught. She wanted to give up. She also started getting nervous thinking about what would happen if this whole thing were a scam. She too feared the wolves ahead and the tigers behind.

I desperately wanted to help Da Mei, so I asked my mother if she could lend me some money. My mother gave me ¥10,000 ($1,250US). I gave it to Da Mei, and she was able to borrow the rest from the bank. I was so happy that day for her and for both of us.

We made a phone call to the agency and asked if we could pay everything at once since getting to Nan Tong was not easy and we didn't want to make two trips. They said yes, so we took all of our money to Nan Tong to pay the fee. It was on a Monday in November, 1999. We didn't go to work that day.

Once we paid the ¥28,000 fee, we got more information. We were told that ¥3,000 of the fee was a deposit which we could lose under certain conditions. For example, if we stayed on Saipan longer than three years, we would lose our deposit. If we got pregnant and had a child, we would lose the money. If we filed a case against a factory or employer, we would lose the money.

They told us that compared to China, the prices on Saipan were higher, so we should buy our necessities—things like soap, shampoo, toothpaste and toothbrushes—to take with us. They then said we should wait for their call to let us know when we were scheduled to go.

We both quit our jobs about two weeks later. Every day we went out and bought things for our trip.

We ended up waiting for three months for the phone call. And then it happened. I remember the day well. It was Tuesday, February 1, 2000. It was close to Chinese New Year, and I was at my mother's house for my father's 60th birthday.

A man from the agency called the house, and my mother answered the phone. He asked to speak to me and told me we had to be at Shanghai airport on Thursday, February 3, 2000, just two days later. Someone would be waiting for us at the airport hotel at 6:30 p.m. The flight to Saipan would leave the next morning—Friday, February 4, 2000—at 8:00 a.m.

I was very unhappy about leaving my father's birthday celebration, but since the bus ride back home was six hours, I had to leave right away. If I waited, by the time I got back home, I would have only one day to get everything together.

Departure Day

Since Da Mei and her husband didn't have a car, and since her house was too far to travel to the airport to get there on time, we agreed that she and her husband would come to my house on Wednesday afternoon—the day before we were to leave—to stay with my husband and me.

We had a family gathering at our house that Thursday. My mother, and my husband's father and mother, my husband's uncle and his wife were there. My father wasn't there—he had to work—but he called us that night to say goodbye. My brother also called from work to say his goodbyes.

Even though it was a family gathering with lots of food, I was too sad to eat. This would be my last night at home.

Our gathering ended early, as we had to leave at 3:00 p.m. that day to go to the airport hotel. My mother was reluctant to let go.

She had started crying a full two days before I was to leave. That day, her eyes were red from crying so much.

"If Saipan is no good, you should come home early. Don't stay," she told me again and again.

My husband's parents were also weeping and sniffling. All their crying started to affect me. I could not control myself. I hugged them crying. My son—at two years old—was too small to understand what was happening, where I was going, or when I would come back. He was the only one not crying.

I really didn't want to leave my son. He is my future. He is my everything, my treasure. However, in China, we say *you should not look at the sky from the bottom of the well*. In other words, you cannot spend your life in one place; you must strive to elevate yourself. We also say *you cannot be a frog in a well*, someone of limited experiences and exposure. I had goals and plans I had to pursue. We also say, *birds die in pursuit of food, and humans die in pursuit of wealth*. That means people will always strive and be enterprising in pursuing matters of importance to them.

As I got inside the car that would take us to the airport, my son suddenly seemed to understand, and started crying too. I felt as if a knife had pierced my heart. Was I being callous and cruel for leaving him?

I asked my neighbor—a good friend who had come to see us off—to look out for my son if he ever needed help.

My father-in-law's friend drove us to Shanghai. My husband and I, and Da Mei, and her husband—the four of us sat silently. Nobody spoke. Everybody had a sad face. Thousands of thoughts. Thousands of emotions. The grief of parting and tearing oneself away. The sadness of separation. It is difficult to describe how miserable I felt. Thousands of words cannot describe the feeling.

It took us ninety minutes to get to Hong Qiao Airport in Shanghai. The hotel was near the airport.

Once outside the hotel, the four of us searched for the words to say our final goodbyes. Da Mei and her husband had soft eyes reflecting such tenderness for each other. The two of them seemed like young lovers. She reminded me of a young girl experiencing her first awakening of love.

My husband told me to come back if things were not good. He said I did not need to hold on to prove anything. He said to remember that I had a son, a mother and a whole family waiting for me. I listened to the words that were coming from his heart, and I felt touched. His eyes were brimming with tears, and at that moment, I forgot all the unhappiness we had been experiencing. Still, I was determined to go ahead with my life.

So, on Friday, February 4, 2000, in the morning, I found myself at China's Shanghai Airport about to start a new life. I was 25 years old. This would be my first time taking a plane. It would be my first time going to another country. It would be my first time leaving my family. Everything about this day of my life was new and curious and hopeful.

Chapter 2:
Don't Stop Until You
Reach the Yellow River ▲

Standing at the front door of the hotel, none of us wanted to say goodbye, but we knew we had to.

Soon, our husbands left, and Da Mei and I walked into the hotel. We saw sixteen other girls there waiting for us. A man from the agency appeared gave us our plane tickets and room numbers. Da Mei and I stayed together on the ground floor.

Our beds were very comfortable, but neither one of us could sleep that night. We stayed up all night talking about the future and waiting for sunrise. It seemed like an eternity of waiting.

We started getting ready at 7:00 a.m. the next morning. We took our showers, had breakfast in the hotel restaurant, and then went back to our room to get our suitcases.

At 8:30 a.m., all eighteen of us walked the few hundred feet from the hotel to the airport, carrying our bags, led by the man from the agency. We checked in for our flight, and within a half-hour we boarded a China-Eastern Airlines flight to Korea.

Nobody could imagine how I was feeling as I sat on that plane. I felt I was in a dream. It just didn't seem real. I was on a flight with seventeen other girls from different cities in China, on our way to work and start new lives in a foreign country many of us had only recently heard of. This was my first time on a plane and my first time leaving home. I couldn't believe it was really happening. I looked out the window. All I could see were clouds.

All the other girls on the plane were from the same province —Jiang Shu, but from different cities. Most were from Nan Tong since that was where the agency was located. Da Mei was from Chang Zhou, and I am from Wu Xi.

During the flight, we talked about where we were from. We asked each others' ages. We got to know each other.

Hong was a fat girl from Nan Tong. She was 18 years old. Her parents were divorced. She lived with her mother and stepfather, but her relationship with them was not good. That's why she was going to Saipan.

Yun was 35 years old, and also from Nan Tong. She had a son. She had her own business in China—a restaurant—but she didn't like the business. She thought that by going to Saipan, she would be able to make more money than she could in China.

Xiao Ran was a single girl from the country part of Nan Tong. She and her parents worked on a farm with her five sisters and brothers. They were poor. She borrowed money from the bank and from friends to be able to go to Saipan. She told me that when she got to Saipan, she would make enough money to pay the bank, pay her friends, and send money back home.

Yan was single and about 20 years old. She was from Bao Ying, a country town also in Jiang Shu province. She had a brother. Her father was a habitual gambler, known to idle away his time in pleasure-seeking and whoring. She told me every time when her father lost money, he would come home angry and hit her mother, her brother and her too. Every day, bill collectors would come to her house asking for payment. Seeing her mother in such a pitiful state —extremely worried, living cautiously and anxious every day— broke her heart. She wanted to make money to help her father pay his debts, and give her mother a better life.

Huan was divorced. Her husband was gluttonous and lazy. That's why she divorced him. She had a son who was only one year old. She gave her son to her mother to take care of while she went to Saipan. It was for her baby, and for herself, that she decided to go.

Lan was about 27 years old. She had short hair and was very fat—about 160 pounds. When she walked her butt shook in a funny way. I called her "Pang Zhi"—which means "fat one." *

*In China, just about everyone has a nickname. On Saipan, because my skin is darker, they call me "Hei Mei" which means "black little sister."

Lan did farm work. She didn't have any way to earn more money. She wanted money to buy a house. She told me the fee to go to Saipan was too high for her. She had to borrow all of it. She was also scared that this whole thing was a con, but she was a risk taker, and was willing to take a chance that things would work out well.

In life, if you decide you want something, you have to be unyielding to realize your goal. In China we say, *don't stop until you reach the Yellow River*, which means never give up until you reach your goal. All of us on that flight, leaving our lives in China for a new life on Saipan, were doing just that.

The entire flight to Korea was about four hours. We landed at about 2:00 p.m. As we made our way through the airport, we could not understand the Korean and English signs. We felt like fools. We stayed in the airport waiting for six hours for our connecting flight. It was very boring in the airport. We just sat, chatted, and waited.

At about 8:00 p.m., we got on a plane that would take us directly to Saipan, but we had made a huge mistake. Because we didn't understand the language or the signs, and no one in our group spoke even a little English or Korean, we ended up getting on the wrong plane. Fortunately the flight attendants checked our tickets, and told us just in time. We left quickly—all eighteen of us rushed off the plane—and someone showed us where the right flight was.

The flight from Korea to Saipan was about four hours; and at about 1:30 on the morning of Saturday, February 5, 2000, we landed on the island of Saipan, CNMI*. We were closer to the Yellow River!

Saipan

On the morning we arrived on Saipan, it was raining. Mirage Factory—where we would be working—sent someone to meet us at the airport. As I sat in the car on the way to my new home, I could smell the soil and the flowers and grass. We saw trees and exotic flowers along the way.

---

*CNMI=Commonwealth of the Northern Mariana Islands.

But it was not like I imagined it at all. At times, the car traveled along very bumpy, unpaved roads. The houses were simple and crude. It was not like the big American city I imagined. It looked very poor. I am not a rich person, but where I was from in Wu Xi seemed richer. And it was very hot on Saipan. Too hot. It felt as if my dream was starting to melt.

It was about 3:00 a.m. by the time we arrived at the Mirage Factory barracks. Once there, I discovered that I and the other girls would be living eight people to a room. Inside our barracks room, there were ten beds—five bunk beds. My bed was up on a top bunk. There was no air conditioning, and only one fan.

"How could I live here with no air conditioning?" I thought to myself as we settled in to our strange new home.

Chapter 3: Factory Life ▲

February 7, 2000 to August 20, 2001

My First Day

The next day—actually, later that day—was a Saturday. Our new roommates awoke angry at Da Mei and me for coming in and waking them up in the middle of the night with the sound of our suitcases. They were not friendly to us at all.

Soon, the barracks manager took all eighteen of us to show us the dining room, the shower facilities, and the factory floor. They told us what time we had to show up to the dining hall to eat, and that if we showed up late, there would be no food for us.

We asked why we could not start working right away. They told us that it was the weekend, and we would start working on Monday morning. So we went back to our barracks to wait.

It would be two days before we would start work in the factory. Those two days wore on like years.

The Barracks

Life as a garment factory worker in the Mirage factory barracks was not like anything you can imagine. There were hundreds of people working at one time, eating at one time, showering at one time, all working overtime all at the same time. After the day's work, we returned to the barracks. Every room was small, and they all were like sheds.

The sun in Saipan is scorching hot. The beds were just wooden frames covered with bamboo sleeping mats. At night, the bed was also hot, like steam—so hot that I could not sleep. We would pour water on the beds to make them cool enough to sleep. We did that every night, just so we could be comfortable.

Other companies had air conditioning. Mirage used bamboo sheets. Wet bamboo. That was our air conditioning!

There were eight people in our room, and only one fan. You couldn't always feel the breeze from the fan. The room walls were made of wood, and very thin. You could hear everything that was happening, every conversation, and every sound...and every room was noisy. There was no privacy.

And then, there were the ants! There were lots of ants living with us in the barracks. Before I went to sleep each night, I had to check the bed and brush them off.

And then, there were the rats. There were always lots of rats running back and forth in the barracks. Sometimes you would be asleep, and a rat would come right up to your face. It was scary. I couldn't sleep with the sound of the running rats, or the fear that they would crawl all over me.

And then, there were the generators. The generators—which provided electricity for the barracks—ran all day and all night. My room was right next to the generator, and was shaking all the time. It was like the sound of thunder in the rooms. It felt like a constant earthquake. I couldn't sleep.

Just about everything about factory life—the rooms, the food, the sleeping, and the showering—yes, just about everything was uncomfortable.

The Food

The food in the Mirage barrack's cafeteria was pig food. It was not cooked well at all. There was often no oil in the food. They didn't want to spend the money. They used a lot of MSG*. Every week, the food was the same. It was always meat. I would sometimes see ants and hair in the soup. We called the cafeteria "dinner hell."

The small amount of food they gave us could not fill my stomach. I would always get hungry. In the morning, if you got up too late, there would be no food for you. I had to start buying my own food to cook and take to work.

---

*MSG: **MonoSodium Glutamate**, also known as "aji no moto": a known carcinogen used to add flavor to food.

The Showers

We showered in communal showers with no doors on the stalls. With so many girls finishing work at the same time, sometimes you had to wait on line for one or two hours just to take a shower. Sometimes we would work until 2:00 a.m. So, sometimes it was so late, and the lines were so long, that we couldn't get to shower before bed. In China, you don't sleep in a clean bed with a dirty body, so we'd sleep on the floor—with the ants and the rats and the rumble of the generators—until the next morning when we could shower. The conditions were disgusting.

The Fights

Throughout the barracks, it seemed there was always someone fighting. Someone was always being scolded. Dinnertime, shower time, rest time, holiday time, work time, any time. And what they were fighting about was *chicken feathers and garlic skins*—petty things, trivial things, things of no importance.

There was fighting in the shower. Because the lines for the shower were so long, some of the girls would give their stalls to their other friends who didn't want to wait on line, causing fights.

At lunchtime, when the bell rang, we had to punch out on the time clock before we went to the cafeteria. If you weren't fast enough, you would arrive at the end of a long line. Some people didn't like to wait, so they tried to cut the line. Other people would get angry, but the cutters didn't care. More fighting.

There was fighting at dinnertime. Everyone wanted to be first to get served. If you were on the end of the line, by the time you got served, there would be little or nothing left. More fighting.

Sometimes there would be no place to sit in the cafeteria, so girls gave their seats to their friends who came late. More fighting.

This would happen every single day. Sometimes when people would fight, the boss would suspend them for two days, sometimes for one week.

I worked at Mirage and lived in their barracks for one-and-a-half years. In all that time, I never had a quiet moment. My life was like the ocean, always churning, never calm. I hoped that in time things would get better, but they never did.

No Outlet

The rooms in the barracks did not have electrical outlets. Every year, during June, July and August, it would get very hot on Saipan. We would request an outlet to plug in our fans. The boss would simply ignore us.

With no electricity, even if we wanted to listen to radios or watch television, we could not. It was very boring every day.

We wanted to get out and do things, but the factory used its authority to intimidate us. They made it clear to us that they didn't want us to go beyond the barracks gate. We were told: "Don't go outside. It is not safe. You will get hurt."

They didn't want us to make friends outside of the barracks walls either. They didn't want the girls to have boyfriends. If you had a boyfriend, you might have sex, perhaps have a baby. If you had a baby, the factory would have to pay the medical bills, and they certainly didn't want to spend the money.

So, we didn't go outside. We only stayed in the factory. We had very few choices. It was an uninteresting and tasteless life.

Chapter 4: Mirage ▲

February 7, 2000 to August 20, 2001

Day 1

On Monday morning, two days after we arrived on Saipan, Da Mei and I went to the Mirage cafeteria to have breakfast. We sat together with the sixteen other girls who had been on our flight. Soon, one of the factory monitors took all eighteen of us to the factory floor for us to start working.

There were three floors of workers in Mirage. The eighteen of us were all spread out and assigned to different floors. The monitor for my floor showed me to my machine, told me what I had to do, and how it should be done. She sat at my station and demonstrated.

My job was to sew the hems on a certain style of women's blouse. As she showed me what I had to do, she told me that I had to complete about 1,000 blouses by the end of the day. She also told me that if my work was no good that I would be asked to punch my time card and go home.

Then she stood and told me to do the same thing she had been doing. She watched me as I did. I was very nervous with her watching me like that. When I finished one blouse, she took it and checked it very carefully.

"Good," she said. "Now do another one."

After I sewed six or seven pieces, she said, "Good," and then called to one of the workers who did the quality inspections to check my work.

"Where in China are you from?" the monitor asked me. "How long have you been sewing?"

I told her I had been working in China for five years.

Once I started working, someone would come by my station every hour to check and make sure the work was being done correctly. I probably did one hundred blouses each hour. It was easy for me to meet the quota since I had done this type of work before.

The Factory Hierarchy

In every factory, there is usually (in descending order of power), an owner, a manager, a factory director, an office worker/secretary (one or more; often the director's girlfriend), a "big" monitor, who overseas all the "lines" of workers, and a "small" monitor, who is one of the factory girls like me who has been put in charge of the "line" of girls in which she works.

Each row of workstations is called a line. There were thirty sewing machine stations, and thus thirty girls per line.

There were also different bosses for each department of the factory. There is a different boss for:
1. Washing clothes
2. Packing
3. Cutting
4. Sewing
5. Attaching labels
6. Checking workmanship

Quotas and Tickets

Here is how we filled our quotas.

While we were at our sewing stations, one of the men in the cutting department would bring a cart or bin with a stack of blouses wrapped together in bundles of different quantities, and with a ticket attached to each bundle. The ticket was divided into several sections for each task that had to be performed on the blouses. After we performed a task, we detached and kept the section of the ticket that corresponded to that task. That little stub had written on it the number of pieces worked on, and the task completed. So, after we finished sewing the hems on ten blouses, we would detach a portion of the ticket that would read "10 blouses; hems sewed."

The next batch of clothes might have twenty blouses wrapped together with another ticket attached. When we completed that batch of clothes, we would again separate the corresponding part of the ticket. At the end of the day, every girl would have a set of ticket stubs, one for ten pieces, one for twenty pieces, and so on.

We would then take the stubs home to total how many pieces we finished that day. We would write our name and our employee number (mine was "204") on each stub.

With sometimes as many as eighty stubs to complete, it might take two or more hours to count and write our names on all the stubs. We didn't get paid for the time we spent at home preparing the ticket stubs.

The next day, when we came to work, we would put our bundle of tickets in a special box. Another office worker would count the tickets, check each girl's productivity, and then the big monitor would use these numbers to assign overtime.

Day's End

That first day, we finished at 5:00 p.m. The dining hall wouldn't open until 5:30 p.m. While we waited, Da Mei and I talked about our first day as factory workers on the island of Saipan.

"Was it easy?" I asked her.

"Yes, but here you have to work very fast. And it's too hot."

"The people here aren't friendly at all," I said.

"I don't like our roommates, either," Da Mei agreed.

Da Mei told me that her bunkmate—the one beneath her— would get angry whenever Da Mei made the slightest noise.

"Don't be scared," I said. "If they want to fight, we'll fight! They think because we're new that we are weak."

After dinner, we waited on line, showered and washed our clothes. We counted our tickets and rested. We felt very tired. By 8:00 p.m. that night, we were fast asleep.

The next day, we got up ready to do it again.

Overtime

Everybody in a factory wants to work overtime hours so they can make more money. In a factory, the bosses and monitors used the productivity indicated by the tickets to determine who got overtime and who didn't. If you were a productive worker, you earned the chance to work overtime. If you were slow, you didn't.

In Mirage, if you finished 100% of your quota, you got to work four hours overtime. If you finished 90% of your quota, you would be allowed to work only three hours overtime. However, if you were a slow worker, with no chance of getting overtime, a monitor could intervene and request overtime for you. But, there was a special little secret to getting a monitor to help you like that.

Getting Ahead at Mirage

Mirage was a Hong Kong factory. Everybody knew there was a set of underground rules for surviving in Hong Kong factories. If you knew the rules, you could get ahead.

The first thing to understand is that there are two types of jobs in a factory: ticket jobs and non-ticket jobs. Ticket jobs are jobs like the one I was doing that had a quota requirement. Some ticket jobs are hard, and some ticket jobs are easy.

Sewing the hem on some styles of blouses can be a very difficult ticket job. If you get it wrong, the hem comes out crooked, and you have to pull it out and start over. You would finish less blouses that day. That's not the kind of job you wanted.

An *easy* ticket job might be to attach the designer label to a shirt or dress. I could do 210-220 labels like that every hour. To make that kind of productivity, however, you can't go to the bathroom, stop to drink water, or take any type of break, but it's an easy job that could increase your productivity.

The second type of job is a *non-ticket* job. A non-ticket job doesn't have a quota requirement. Non-ticket jobs include checking if the workmanship is good, sweeping the floors, being the monitor's "secretary," or providing floor assistance (giving needles and thread to the girls working on the lines)—those are the easiest jobs.

If you wanted a non-ticket job, or an easy ticket job, you could get it a few ways at a Hong Kong factory. You could simply bribe the monitor to give you an easier assignment. In Mirage, for example, if you paid the big monitor $500, she could get you an easy job. Some people were very slow workers, but they would always get overtime or easy jobs by paying off the monitor. That made me angry. It was very unfair.

Sometimes, girls would pay a monitor just to leave them alone. You see, if a monitor didn't like you, she could easily make trouble for you. She could tell the boss lies about you. The big monitor and the director went out drinking together, and had a friendly relationship outside of the factory, so they were always on the same side in any dispute. Sometimes it was worth paying the big monitor just to have a stress-free life.

Atu. (Like an Egg Hitting a Rock)

Atu was our big monitor. She was from China, Ling Bo. She was 38 years old, perhaps 40. She was tall, had short hair, and looked like a man. She was cunning, and as cruel as a wolf. She used her position and power to bully others, and she loved money as much as life. She wanted us to give her money, or buy her things. If we did, she would give us better jobs and easier positions.

My character would not allow me to give her money. I don't like to ask other people for favors in that way. I never want to be at the mercy of others or compromise my standards. So, as a result, I would often get very hard work to do.

I remember one morning, Atu and I had a fight. I had been at the factory for two weeks, and had been at work for an hour. Atu came to my work area and gave me some work that was not my assigned task. A girl named Guan usually did it.

Guan had come to the factory three months earlier. She worked very slowly. As a result, Atu had scolded her and made her job and life difficult. Guan decided to do what many slow workers did: she paid Big Monitor $500 to make her life easy. That meant someone else's life would get harder. That someone was me.

Atu wanted me to do Guan's work. I told her no.

"Why do you tell me to do that work?" I asked.

"Don't answer back!" she shouted. "If I tell you to do something, you have to do it! You cannot tell me no!" she fumed.

She put the clothes on my table. I was angry, too. I picked them up, and threw them down on the work area next to me. She picked them up, and put them back on my table. I picked them up again, and when I threw them back to the space next to me, some of them fell on the floor. That made Atu even angrier.

"Stop working now!" she yelled at me. "Take your time card, punch out, and go home!"

She had given me the clothes to work on thinking that since I was new, that I would be too afraid to defy her. For all of my life, I've been temperamental, honest and frank. I march forward courageously. I may look shy, but I don't back down in fear. I don't swallow insults easily. I was resolute. I didn't do it. I was very angry and bursting with words I wanted to say to her.

I had seen that if you didn't do what Atu said, she would send you home and tell you not to come back in the afternoon. Sure enough, as I left, she told me not to come back. Denying a factory girl the chance to make money was the ultimate punishment.

"No matter! I don't care!" I shouted as I left.

So, that afternoon, I didn't go to work. I went to the beach, sat, and watched the waves, and stayed there for the rest of the day.

My friends told me later that my fighting with Atu was *like an egg hitting a rock.* They said I was asking for trouble by defying her. They reminded me, as we say in China, that *it is easier to dodge an open attack, but much harder to avoid a secret one*, and that next time she might resort to something underhanded— something secretive and harder to see and avoid—to get back at me.

"You know she has power," they warned me. "You shouldn't fight with her. If she wanted to retaliate, it would be as easy for her as turning her hand over."

From that time, just two weeks after my first day of work, my big monitor, Atu, developed a bitter hatred of me.

One day, Atu had a fight with another girl named Xiao Qing. They were both from the same place in China, Ning Bo. Xiao Qing had been on Saipan for five years.

That week, Mirage was helping another factory to fill a large order. The shipping date was approaching, and they needed the work done quickly. We worked fourteen hours every day. The work was very hard—so hard that sometimes the girls were having trouble concentrating and sewing properly.

That day, Atu walked over to Xiao Qing's line, inspected the clothes, and told Xiao Qing, "Your sewing is no good!"

Xiao Qing replied, "It's not only me sewing those clothes. There are five other girls sewing! Why are you only telling me? Is it because I didn't give you money? Is that why? You're just trying to make trouble for me!"

Everybody stopped and stared at Atu and Xiao Qing. We couldn't believe Xiao was being so bold. Their argument continued, getting louder and louder. Atu was becoming more irritated. She threw the spoiled clothes at Xiao Qing.

"Fix them and then go home!" she yelled at Xiao Qing.

Xiao Qing said no.

Atu got angry and told her not to come back for three days!

Xiao Qing started shaking and crying. She threw all the clothes down and shouted, "I want you to go with me to the factory office to see the Assistant Manager!"

Atu refused. She wouldn't let a worker tell her what to do.

"I'm not going!" Atu shouted. "If you want to go, you can go by yourself!"

Xiao Qing ran downstairs to the office crying.

In a few minutes, Mr. Wong, the assistant manager, came upstairs to Atu's area.

"What's happening?" he asked

"Xiao Qing's work is no good!" Atu told him. "She's sewing a lot of bad clothes."

Now, the reality is, if you are a factory girl, whether you're right or wrong, the boss will never agree with you since you are only a worker. He will always take the side of the big monitor.

"If everybody behaves like you and fights with the monitor," Mr. Wong began, scolding Xiao, "then every day here would be *like chickens and dogs living together.*"

Mr. Wong talked to Atu for a few minutes, and then turned to talk to Xiao Qing. Just as Atu had done, he told her not to come back for three days, and to write a self-criticism letter asking for the monitor's forgiveness. She also had to sign a warning letter—it was her first. If you got over three warning letters, you would be fired and sent back to China. Most Hong Kong factory bosses are cruel as wolves. They all breathe through the same nostrils.

Xiao Qing stayed in the barracks for three days, and slept. She was too angry to eat. After her sentence was over, she came back to work. She looked drawn. She had lost a lot of weight.

She didn't talk to Atu after that. She never talked with anyone about the argument, or what happened that day. She would simply come in, do her work for the day, and leave.

This sort of thing happened a lot. It happened to Pang Zhi (the fat one), too. When she came to Saipan, the boss told her to work on the second floor. The second floor big monitor was A Fang. Atu and A Fang were good friends. She, too, had short hair. In fact, she looked just like Atu, and they acted the same. For the two of them, money was like air. They would do anything for it.

Because Pang Zhi was fat, her work was not as productive. She was awkward, and she wasn't as nimble as the rest of us. She was only allowed to work eight hours with no overtime. A Fang would give mean looks to Pang Zhi, and scold her repeatedly.

Pang Zhi was too scared to stand up to A Fang. She would get very upset, but would simply go to the barracks and cry. The eighteen of us who came to Saipan at the same time couldn't always find someone we could talk to when things got rough. So we all became friends and supporters in adversity. Whether happy or sad, we would be there for each other.

A year later, we heard that Pang Zhi's 2-year old daughter in China drowned. Even after her daughter died, Pang Zhi didn't go home. She stayed on Saipan to work for another three years and then went back home. I could only imagine what she was feeling. But not everyone is open with their feelings. Some people's hearts remain a secret.

Yun, the 35-year old who had a business in China—another girl from the plane—was very pretty, and was able to use that to win favor with the bosses. She worked on the first floor on the "B" line.

Her monitor's name was Xue, from China, Chong Qing. Xue was tall and had short hair. Compared to other monitors, she wasn't bad. She seemed content with her life, and wasn't as greedy.

Yun would give food to her monitor, Xue, and often took her out to dinner. Pretty looks can win you favor anywhere. If you're ugly, nobody likes you. Nobody wants to be your friend.

Getting Sick at Mirage

When we got sick while working at Mirage, they would never take us to the hospital. They would only give us some pills.

Every factory had a little room—like a little first aid room —with bandages and a poor stash of medicine for headaches. There was a worker there whose job it was to give you medicine if you got sick. I went there many times and got pills for headaches, or cream for skin rashes. If the "doctor" in that room said you could get a day off, that would be the only time the boss would allow it.

I remember a worker named Ying had been feeling sick for a few days, and could not eat or sleep. She had low blood pressure, and, as the work place was so hot, she was always dizzy and would often faint at work.

I remember one day when we were working together, she fainted. I got very scared and held her in my arms. The other girls came to our assistance, to lend a hand. Five of us stayed with her. Some brought water, some brought small towels, some helped massage her face. After about five minutes, she opened her eyes.

When she realized she was in my arms, she asked, "Why are you carrying me? Why is everybody looking at me?"

We didn't know whether to laugh or cry.

That happened to Ying about five or six times during that year. When it came time for renewal, the monitor told the boss not to renew her contract.

"You're always fainting," Atu told Ying. "You have to go home. We cannot renew your contract again."

Ying didn't want to go home, but she had no choice.

If you found yourself asking for sick leave, or a hospital visit two or three times, they would always ask, "Why are you the only one with problems?" That would make you feel as if your illness was make-believe, and that you were being a burden. If you went to the hospital more than twice for the year, your contract wouldn't be renewed. Because of treatment like this, many people were scared to speak up when they got sick. If you wanted to get renewed for the next year, you had better keep your mouth shut.

Most of us knew this before we arrived. Most girls would bring their own store-bought or herbal medicines from China with them. Others would simply learn to live with whatever was wrong with them rather than risk being sent back to China.

The factories didn't want to spend the money caring for sick workers. If you went to the hospital on your own, you would have to pay the bill yourself. Sometimes a girl would feel sick and simply ask for a day off. The boss would always say no. Cruel as a wolf.

A Factory by Any Other Name

Saipan factories and China factories are very different. In China, there is no day off except Chinese New Year. We work seven days a week, every week, every month, every year. On Saipan, there is always a day off every week, sometimes two!

In one month in China, you could make ¥1,000. On Saipan for a month's work, you could earn as much as ¥6,000.

In China, especially during the cold winters, it's harder to wake up and leave your house. On Saipan, where it's always summer, it's much easier to wake up and go out.

In China, the people who work in a factory are very friendly to each other. Sometimes we would get together and have small parties. On Saipan, people weren't as friendly. There's a big difference in how the Chinese people act here on Saipan. Once they come to work here, they are not as friendly as if we were all in China. One minute they can be smiling and the next not. It's harder to get along with the Chinese girls here.

In China, we would help each other finish each other's work. There is overtime available every day, but most people have families, and want to leave early to go home. In China, no one wants to work overtime. Here on Saipan, since people are here to make as much money as possible, and since overtime is based on productivity, no one wants someone else to help them do their work. Everybody becomes more selfish striving to get overtime.

In China we say *men's hearts differ as much as their faces do*. In other words, there are as many types of behaviors and personalities as there are faces. It's true in China, but here on Saipan, you can't trust everybody. In everything you do, and especially in factory life, you have to be careful. Some people liked to "kiss up" to the boss, and tell untrue stories to win the boss' favor. Outside the factory, people will try to scam you. You have to be very careful here.

In China, after you finish work, you have to buy food, cook, take care of children, and family and housework duties. Here on Saipan, after work, I have time to rest. I can enjoy the single life. I can do anything I want. If I'm hungry, I can cook. If I'm not hungry, I don't have to cook. Things here are not like in China, where I have to cook all the time.

Yes, working on Saipan, so far away from home, makes me homesick a lot, but back home, I'm not as free.

A Friend in the Fire

My brother had a friend named Guang who worked at Mirage factory. Guang and my brother had been very good friends in China. When my brother first found out I was going to Saipan, he wrote to Guang:

> *Dear brother,*
> *How are you? Long time no talk. I don't know how everything is going. My sister is going to Saipan to work. She is young and has never been to another country. Could you take care of her for me?*

After two days on Saipan, I found out that Guang was working at the Mirage factory dining hall cleaning and washing. He had already been on Saipan for four years

I asked him about Mirage, and how much my check would be. He told me it depended on how many hours I worked, but that with overtime, I could be making about $600 each month.

"My first year on Saipan, I made about $8,000," he told me.

His salary was the same each month. He worked ten hours a day—including Saturdays and Sundays—and got paid every two weeks. They deducted $100 each period for food and barracks.

He and I did the math for each bi-weekly paycheck.

10 hours each day x 14 days = 140 hours
80 hours was (regular) x 3.05/hour = $244.00
60 hours was (overtime) x 4.58/hour = $274.80
SUBTOTAL =$518.80
less about $70 deducted for taxes= $448.80
less $100 deducted for food and barracks=$348.80
TOTAL: $348.80/two weeks

Guang was making $348 every two weeks, or about $700 each month. He said the salary was not bad, but his monitor—who was from China, An Hui—was no good. He told me everybody was from An Hui except him. Because of that, he got assigned the hard and dirty work. He told me the situation with his monitor was very bad. When he told me about it, I could see tears in his eyes. He was unhappy, but from his perspective, he said he didn't have a choice.

"If you stay here, you have to learn to be patient, and bide your time," he told me. "If you can wait things out, everything will go smoothly, and could be as boundless as the sea and sky. If someone talks bad about you, don't get angry. Just walk away."

Now that I had been on Saipan for a few weeks, I was beginning to understand. After just a few days on Saipan, I had already felt a sadness and a longing to go home. I missed my parents and my son. Saipan was not like I envisioned it. My great plans and aspirations disappeared and were destroyed completely.

Every day, I was depressed, sad, worried, homesick, lonely and regretful. I felt as if there were invisible shackles, almost like a heavy weight pressing down upon me. At night, my tears ran like raindrops. Many times I felt like going back home. Many times I thought about giving up.

I had never tasted being so home sick. I felt so lonely that I cried every night. I couldn't sleep. When people started talking about China, my tears would not stop.

I felt like hitting myself. I regretted not listening to my family. I shouldn't have come. I shouldn't have been so rash.But, then I thought about the fees and expenses I paid to get here, and that it had only been a few weeks, and I hadn't made any money. I couldn't go home. If I did, my friends would laugh at me.

Other girls didn't see it the same way. Many girls gave up, and asked the boss to buy their tickets and send them back to China. The boss didn't really care one way or another. If one person didn't like it, there would always be someone else in China who was willing to come to Saipan to work.

This was life at Mirage. Our boss was always threatening us. If we didn't work fast, or if we weren't doing good work, he threatened to send us back to China. Everyday, we had to finish our quota. If not, we risked being sent back. It was very tiring and stressful work. I felt I was going crazy. In fact, some people did.

Yes, there were girls literally going crazy from all the pressure and stress. Because of the fighting, some would sleep with scissors under their pillows to feel safe. Some wouldn't eat. Some couldn't sleep. Others disappeared for three or four days at a time, to get a break. When the boss found them, they got sent back to China.

Some people gave money to the monitors to get better jobs and a stress-free life. But we were new there, so we didn't have money yet. There were some girls who had been there so long that they're character was old. Everyday their faces were long, and unfriendly. Every day, they thought of ways to bully the new workers. I just didn't understand that. I believe that people from all corners of the world can all get along. In life, there's only one chance. Why not act like friends and family?

There were many times I thought about going back to China, but I had made a promise to myself and to my family. I had to keep going. I couldn't give up. I told myself that if other people could do it, that I could too.

Life has many stages and levels. Sometimes you have to take on different roles to survive. Life has many tastes. If you don't taste the sour, you won't get to taste the sweet.

$30,000US was my goal, so I had to stay. I wanted a better life so I could buy a house, and perhaps start my own business. I wanted a car. I wanted to take care of my family, and send my son to a good school in China. I had not yet reached the Yellow River, so I refused to stop.

*****

Now that I was here for two weeks, I wanted to tell my family that I had arrived safely on Saipan. I borrowed $5.00 from Guang, bought a phone card, and called my mother and father.

Our conversation was short, because the phone card gave me only thirty minutes of time to talk. Every time we called we had to think about the cost.

"Is everything good there?" they asked.

I wanted to tell them it was terrible, that I was scared and lonely, and that the people weren't nice, but I decided I didn't want my mother and father to worry about me.

"Everything is great!" I said. "The only problem is that I miss home."

That first call back home lasted only two minutes. I couldn't talk longer, because I had to think about the money. I was always comparing the exchange rate in my head making sure I didn't spend more than I had to.

"Family Happiness"

Everybody has a need for warmth, companionship and love. Whether man or woman, everyone has a tender spot in the rooms of their hearts. When you feel lonely, or melancholy or frustrated, or live in desperate times, you need spiritual support, and some escape from worry. You need someone to listen to you, to understand you, to share life's sorrows as well as its joys. Everybody has the same seven emotions*, and experiences the same sensory pleasures. People can't control their needs and desires.

As factory workers, we were all in the same boat—living a hard life, far away from home. So, it was only natural that men and women got together for comfort.

In Traditional Chinese Medicine, the emotions are considered the major internal cause of disease. The seven emotions are Joy, Anger, Anxiety Pensiveness, Grief, (chronic) Fear and (sudden) Fright.

However, in China, many people have old ideas. People frown upon a man and woman living together if they are not married. It causes much gossip and judgment. If you're living together and not husband and wife, you're judged as immoral.

In China, as well, certain things are to be done in private. However, the younger girls with more western culture influence, don't have the same respect for Chinese morality, propriety and dignity. As the time away from home grew longer, people did things that they would not dream of doing in China.

Some girls would move in to their boyfriends' rooms in the barracks. Now remember, that in the barracks, a man might be sharing a room with seven other men. Remember, also, that the beds are bunk beds in both the men's and women's quarters.

So, you might have a case where a couple sleeps together in a bunk bed, making the bed shake and squeak at night. It is difficult for their bunkmates below them, and their roommates to sleep. Wouldn't you agree?

Every man wants to have a girlfriend. Some men have girlfriends. Some do not. The ones without girlfriends get jealous, depressed and angry as a result. If *you* saw that every day, how would *you* feel? Some men couldn't take it. They would go to the office and ask if they could change rooms.

One day there was a big scandal in the factory involving a girl who worked in my line. Her name was Xiao Yan. She was 20 years old, skinny and tall. Her hair was short like a boy's. She was a pretty girl, but she was loose. We all knew that she had at least two boyfriends, and one was the factory boss himself! But this scandal involved her and Da Zhang, a man in the cutting department.

It happened about 9:00 a.m. while everybody was at work. Xiao Yan and Da Zhang were the only two who didn't show up at work that day. Xiao Yan had gone to Da Zhang's barracks to enjoy "family happiness" with him. Maybe Xiao Yan and her boyfriend were *too* happy and forgot to lock the door.

Now, in the factory, the cleaning people worked every day. They had keys to all the barracks.

In China, we say, *without coincidences, there would be no stories.* Just when they got naked, the cleaning woman came through the door, and saw them! She didn't know what to do. She watched for a few seconds, and then ran away. By noon that day, she had told her friend. That friend told another and another. The story spread quickly! It caused a big excitement in the factory.

By five o'clock, everybody on all three floors on all the lines knew. The news might have spread quicker, but we were all working hard to make our quotas! The cleaning woman also added her own details about what she saw to the story to make it spicier.

The next day, when Xiao Yan came to work. Everybody looked at her. She knew that we all knew. She couldn't keep her head up. In China, we say that things like that offend public decency. It was not a good thing to be involved in such a scandal.

This was really bad for Xiao Yan. In China, if you accidentally see two people having sex it's bad luck for you too. But it was also bad for Xiao Yan. She lost face. She lost moral standing.

You might think people would forget. But, in China, people never forget. In China, we believe that to be the subject of gossip is a fearful thing to be avoided at all costs. People laugh at you for a long time. Once something like this gets out, you cannot take it back. It can affect you mentally, as well, to be the constant target of such ridicule and loss of respect.

This would affect Xiao Yan's life for a long time. Over the next few weeks, she became depressed and withdrawn. About a month later, she went back to China. She couldn't stay on Saipan.

I Hate Machine Men!

The machine maintenance men at the factory were sickening. For some reason, almost every single one of them was haughty and self-important, and acted like they were royalty. Their job was to fix our sewing machines when they broke, but you always had to call them many times before they would come to help. It was very frustrating, because we were all hurrying to make our quotas. If they didn't come to fix our broken machines quickly, the monitors would scold us, and we might not get overtime.

We prayed that our machines wouldn't break down, but many of those machines were undependable.

There was one machine man from Guang Xi who had been on Saipan for five years. He was very proud of himself. He looked down on the factory workers, and especially despised new workers like me. There was a small room in the factory where he stayed. When we went to him to ask him to fix our machines, he would always do things to delay and frustrate us.

"Go back and clean your machine, change your needle and change your thread. See if that works first," he would say, as if it was something simple wrong with the machine, and we didn't know better. He did that on purpose, to waste our time. After you finished cleaning, you would have to go back to ask him again.

"Okay, okay, I'm coming," he would say impatiently.

Then you would go back to your station and wait. Twenty minutes. Thirty minutes. It was frustrating. For workers, time is money. We knew he was just being mean.

However, if a pretty girl came to ask to fix her machine, he would run faster than a rabbit to help her. I would be sitting waiting after having called him two or three times over the course of an hour, and then see him running to fix another girl's machine.

When the new girls got together to talk about him, we all agreed that we hated him.

If we were sitting at our machines waiting for the machine man, Atu would scold us. She would blame us for not being productive. Sometimes I would cry.

If we asked Atu to use her authority to get the machine men to come to fix our machines, she would scold us even more.

"Why can't you go yourself?" Atu would ask. "It's your machine! Get it fixed!"

Even now, when I think about it, I still feel like I could hit him if I could. I hate machine men!

My First Paycheck!

On February 20, 2000, two weeks after I arrived on Saipan, I got my first paycheck! It was for about $210US. That was about ¥1,680. This was the first time I ever received so much money.

A few days after we had first started working, the factory boss brought the bank worker from the Bank of Saipan to the office to help everyone start an account. So, the money had been directly deposited into our accounts.

The check was for two weeks' work. In China, I could buy a 21-inch color television for about ¥1,000. I could buy a washing machine for ¥600. An air conditioner could cost ¥2,000. My rent in China was about ¥180. That apartment was owned by my in-laws, so we had gotten it at a good price. It was actually worth about ¥400 per month. My son's school fee was ¥200 each month.

Yes, my first paycheck! I was very happy. Getting our checks made things a little better for many of us new girls at Mirage. It gave us some hope for the future. The eighteen of us who had come at the same time got together and talked about our checks, and to compare the values of the US dollar and Chinese yuan.

That night, I called my mother and father to share the good news. When I told them how much money I had earned, they agreed that it was good. They asked me how much I paid in taxes. They said that it was better than in China.

I was earning the equivalent of about ¥3,300 per month. At that time in China, bosses were making ¥3,500 per month. They told me that if I could make ¥4,500 per month, I would be doing better than what even the *managers* in China were making.

We were getting checks every two weeks. That made us very happy. After about three months, we started buying drinks, and some food to cook. We didn't have to haggle over every penny. We didn't have to deprive ourselves. Sometimes we would buy noodles and biscuits and vegetables to cook for ourselves since the barracks food was no good. Sometimes we would get hungry after working overtime. Da Mei and I would cook together in our room on a little portable butane can stove we bought for ten dollars.

After about six months, Da Mei and I started to send money back to China to repay what we had borrowed.

From the beginning, many girls didn't like to spend their money—not even a single dollar if they could manage it.

Da Mei and I were able to save a little extra for the first few months since we had brought many things from China. We didn't have to buy clothes, shampoo or soap, not even tissues and feminine pads. I remember people at the airport laughed at us when they checked our bags and saw the toilet paper and pads.

I was spending about ten or twenty dollars every month—saving everything else. I spent about $700 my first year. Da Mei spent only about $200. She could really hold on to a dollar. She liked to eat, but didn't like to buy. I started to think she was a bit selfish—always wanting me to spend *my* money for both of us. Sometimes we would get angry and stop talking. After three or four months, we stopped spending time together.

When people come to Saipan to work, not everyone is successful at saving their money to send to their families or to take back to China. Some lose it in many ways. I'm thinking, specifically, about the "Long City Traders Scam."

The Long City Traders Scam

I had been on Saipan for about six months. I had repaid the people I had borrowed money from, and I had $2,000 in a Long City Traders account.

Long City was actually a jewelry store located in Garapan. It was also an employment agency and remittance company. You could also save your money with them. Because their interest rate was higher than the bank's, many of the girls kept their money there and lived on the interest which they withdrew every month.

When I arrived on Saipan, Long City had already been operating for four or five years. People trusted them. Many girls withdrew all their money from the banks and kept it instead at Long City. So, just like many of the girls working on Saipan, I put my $2,000 into Long City so I could earn more interest.

One day, in August or September of 2000, I phoned my mother and happened to tell her about my Long City account.

"That's not safe," she told me. "Don't trust them, and don't keep your money there. You don't know men's hearts."

She told me to take my money out of Long City.

"I'm not the only one with money there," I argued. "Some people even have $20,000 there."

"Other people is other people," she argued back. "Take your money out!" she said again.

I wasn't exactly happy about it, but I had to listen to my mother. So, about a week later, I went to Long City and withdrew my money.

Then, something totally unexpected happened. About two weeks later, without notice, the store suddenly closed.

For the first two days, everybody thought that maybe the owners were simply taking a vacation. Nobody thought that much about it. After all, they'd been in business for four or five years.

But, by the third day, it started to seem unusual. In all the years they had been operating, they had never been closed for three straight days. People started to worry.

Some of the girls used their work hours to go to the store to see what was really happening. All they could see was a closed door. You could see through the glass that there were still some jewelry items visible, but much of the valuables were gone.

Nobody could believe it. Someone called the police. News spread quickly. It fast became a sensation.

It wasn't only Mirage workers like me who kept their money there. L&T factory workers and others from all over Saipan were included. As crowds gathered outside the store, rumors started.

"I heard the owner ran away," one said.

"Maybe it will open again," said another. "It's only been three days."

Workers from several factories waited all day outside the store hoping someone would show up. A few of the men spent all night there, not wanting to miss the owner's appearance. *If not during the day, then perhaps at night the owners may show up.*

As the reality of what was happening set in, many of the girls got so depressed and scared, that they couldn't work anymore. Some didn't show up at work for weeks. Some couldn't eat.

Others tried to console them. "It's already gone," they told them. "You have to eat. You have to start again."

The boss also felt very bad for the workers. He visited the barracks to give advice, console us, and offer encouragement.

"You have to be strong," he told them. "When you lose something, you just have to start again."

I was lucky to take my money out just in time, but I was sympathetic. All that sweat and toil. Night after night, week after week, month after month, year after year of overtime, lost. Years of careful calculation and strict budgeting, economizing on food and clothing to save as much as possible, lost.

I know one girl, Xiao Lang, who, for an entire year, spent only $150. She never bought a thing she didn't need. I couldn't believe that she could live an entire year and spend only $150. Every day, she would eat only the factory food, as bad as it was. She never once bought anything from the stores. When you looked at her you could tell she was malnourished. Three years of diligent savings were all with Long City. It was probably about $27,000.

Xiao Lang was at work when she heard the news about Long City. She passed out and fell on the floor by her machine. The monitor called the director who took her to the hospital. About a half-hour later, she woke up. She could only cry. No one will ever understand how she felt. All her money was gone, never to be retrieved. Every single penny.

Two men and a boss worked at that store. The boss was over 40. The two young men were about 25. They were all from Hong Kong. Everybody was angry and sad at the heartless actions of these men. They were Chinese. How could they do that to their own people?

Now, the newspapers on Saipan reported the amount lost at $100,000, but that was completely wrong. Even the same newspaper stated that one girl alone had $35,000 in savings, and I personally knew of others who had $10,000, and $20,000 each. Husbands and wives had their savings there. Factory workers who had worked many years on Saipan had their entire life's savings there.

The newspapers also reported that more than 700 people had been scammed. It was many more than that. Now, think about it. Even if it *was* only 700 people, and even if those 700 had only a small $2,000 saved like I did, the total figure would already be over 1.4 million dollars! We factory workers knew that the amount was in the millions, perhaps closer to ten million dollars stolen.

Even though it was sad, there was a lesson to be learned from what happened at Long City. Sometimes when you lose money like that, you can't only blame the thief. Those girls were unwise to give everything they had to Long City in the hopes of getting that little advantage in interest.

Many weeks after the incident, people were still suffering, still unhappy and still crying over their loss.

The government and the police were very helpful. They circulated information about the owner. A few weeks later, they caught the two store workers at the airport attempting to leave the island. The workers said the boss didn't tell them he was leaving, that they were just as surprised by his actions as everyone else, and were just as much victims—now with no jobs—as everybody else.

The police didn't believe them, and took them to the station. We never found out what happened to them.

Even now, nine years later, the owner has never been caught. But nobody escapes the judgment of heaven. I hope and believe one day he will be caught, for he's a sinful man, guilty of a crime for which even his death cannot atone. He had stolen so many people's dreams of a better life, their futures, their families' survival, their children's education, medicine for the sick—so much.

One girl named Hui—she looked to be about 35 years old— had just sent $18,000 to China through Long City two days before they closed. When she heard that the store had closed, she turned into a different person. She seemed to lose her mind. She cried every day. She phoned China three or four times a day hoping that her parents in China had received the money. They never did.

She would talk about nothing else all day. She would cry constantly. She wouldn't work. She went out alone every night, and no one knew where she went.

The boss got very scared. He called Hui's parents in China to let them know what had happened at Long City, and how strangely she had been behaving since then.

Hui's parents asked the boss to buy her ticket back to China. They were scared something bad would happen to her. Eventually, Hui went back to China, and we never saw her again.

When I called and told my mother what happened, she was shocked.

"Did you take your money out?" she asked worriedly.

"Yes," I told her.

"See? You have to listen to me," she said. "You don't ever really know how people think, and what they will do."

She was right. I had been lucky.

Men and Gambling

Scams like Long City weren't the only traps people fell into. The men from China are another good example of how people lose their money on Saipan.

A man, even if he's not particularly handsome, wants to have a girlfriend. The men believe they have to buy things to make the girls happy, so they gamble as a way to make more money.

They take their chances at the many poker houses on Saipan. Every two weeks, when their paycheck comes, it's quickly spent on girls and gambling.

I have a friend from China, Chong Qing, named Ying. Her boyfriend on Saipan was 22 years old. When he first came to Saipan, he was a good man. Two short months later, however, he started gambling.

Every night he would go with the older workers in the packing department—those who had been on Saipan for many years —to the poker houses. After the third or fourth time, he soon became addicted. With every paycheck, his first thought was to take it to the poker room. It didn't matter what time he finished work.

Sometimes, after working many hours of overtime, he would finish at 2:00 a.m. or 3:00 a.m., but it wouldn't matter. He would head straight for the poker rooms. It wouldn't matter the weather either, he would be there religiously. He would play all night until it was time to go back to work. Needless to say, he lost all of his money.

But, he didn't learn. He would get frustrated and angry, and would always try to win back what he lost. He borrowed from his friends and co-workers, and even his girlfriend, Ying.

Ying would try to give him advice and convince him to change his ways. "That money is what you paid to learn a lesson," she told him.

For gamblers, however, their strongest habit is their promise to change. Even if you tied him down with a rope, he would find a way. A day without gambling is like death for an addict. He would promise her he would stop, but when the paycheck would come, he would disappear again to the poker house.

Ying told me that he first borrowed $50 to use to win back what he lost. He lost the $50, and came back the same day to borrow $50 more. She gave him $100. He went back to the poker room, and lost that too. He came back and asked for more, but this time she told him no. So, he borrowed $50 from another girl friend, and this time he won $1,000! When he won, he was angry with Ying for not lending him more money when he had asked *her*, so he bought drinks and food for the other girl who lent him the money, and never paid Ying back her $150. After that happened, he stopped talking to Ying.

Because he gambled so much at all hours of the night and morning, he would be tired all day, and would always make mistakes at work. Even the packing boss talked to him about it, but with no success. So, when his two-year contract expired, the factory didn't renew it. When he went back to China, he didn't have one dollar to his name, and he owed many people money.

He was ashamed to go back to China in such a state. He had stayed two years and had nothing to show for it.

Unfortunately, many of the Chinese men on Saipan ended up in a similar situation.

Xiao Yang

Xiao Yang is another friend of mine from Wu Xi. He had been on Saipan four years before I arrived. He, too, worked in the packing department at Mirage. He was a hardened gambler who would stop at nothing to win.

Xiao Yang was at the poker house every day. If he didn't go on a particular day, he couldn't sleep. After five years working every day, he too didn't have any money, and owed many others.

However, Xiao Yang had a wife and children back in China, and in all the years he'd been here, he hadn't sent a single penny back to them.

"I don't have any money," he would tell his wife.

"Where's the money going?" she would ask.

"Somebody borrowed it," he would lie.

She threatened to separate and divorce him if things continued, but that didn't affect him. He still continued to gamble.

True to her word, we soon found out that his wife in China left him, but he still didn't seem to care. It was not enough reason to change his ways. No wife? No problem. No children? No problem. No poker? *Big* problem! The only thing that mattered in his life was poker—not his wife, nor his children. Giving up gambling would be the only problem he really recognized. After five years, he too was as poor as a church mouse.

Tsunami!

Factory life dragged on with each day being just like the one before. Work. Barracks. Work. Barracks. Then one day, on the evening of November 3, 2000, we heard that a tsunami was coming.

Only the "local" girls—those born on Saipan—knew just how dangerous a tsunami could be. In all the years I was growing up in China, I had never heard of nor seen one, and never knew how dangerous it could be. So, when I heard the news, it didn't really matter to me. I wasn't scared. However, when other people in the factory started talking about what they knew or heard, they all looked so fearful and sad, I started to get scared too.

It must have been serious, because the factory boss let us finish early that day. He told everyone to stay indoors for our safety. He, however, took the factory bus, loaded up the director, big monitors, and manager and went to higher ground. Some of the girls who had friends around Saipan, and those who had cars, also left the barracks. Those of us without any friends outside the barracks—the new girls—simply had to stay where we were.

In our room, only Da Mei and I were left. The six other girls were gone. We took our bank books, and passports and placed them in our bags and kept them with us at all times. Outside the barracks, we heard people discussing just how bad a tsunami could be.

Some were saying that when a tsunami came, all of Saipan would be covered, and all that would be left where Saipan used to be would be a vast expanse of water.

When we heard what our fate would be, we regretted ever coming to Saipan. We were young. We had children. We had parents. We didn't want to die. Furthermore, we didn't want to die in a foreign country so far away from our families. We hugged each other and cried.

As we hugged each other, we heard noises outside getting louder. We saw people fleeing. Cars packed the roads. People were blowing their horns. Sirens were blaring. Police were going to people's homes, and over loudspeakers, and were advising people not to stay at home, but to move to higher ground.

Da Mei and I went back to our room in the barracks more afraid than before. We pulled our suitcases out, and put on our sneakers, just in case we had to do some fast fleeing ourselves.

It was a freakish, chilling time. Old folks in China always say that animals can tell whenever natural disasters like earthquakes and storms are approaching. That day, the roosters and dogs around the barracks were making more noise than usual. They barked and crowed all day and all night. They never stopped. People shouting. Horns blowing. Dogs barking. Roosters crowing. It made the whole experience much more frightening and strange.

Back in the barracks, Da Mei and I comforted each other.

"Do you want to call China and let them know what's happening?" Da Mei asked. "If something happens to us, at least they'll know."

It was a good idea. So we went to a telecom store to make a call. We discovered there were many people waiting to call their families back home too. People from Thailand, the Philippines, Bangladesh, and Sri Lanka were there too. We waited almost half hour. As I waited, I thought about it more. I really didn't want my family to worry about me, but Da Mei convinced me that it was best for them to know what was happening.

My mother picked up the phone.

"Tonight there might be a tsunami, but we're not sure yet."

"What is a tsunami?" my mother asked.

"It's a big ocean wave. It's very dangerous. If it comes, everything will be washed away, and we'll all die."

As I talked to her, my voice cracked. I choked back tears and I couldn't speak. I felt that this was the last time I would hear my mother's voice again.

My mother started crying. I didn't want to hang up the phone. I wanted to console her.

"Take care of yourself," I told her. "I'll be alright. Don't worry about me. I'm sure it will be alright. Nothing will happen."

My mother gave the phone to my brother. We said our goodbyes. The entire call lasted about five minutes. Afterwards, Da Mei called her family.

When we were finished, we went back to our room. It was about 11:30 p.m. My body was shaking from fear, and cold.

Mirage had three buildings being used as barracks. One was on the factory compound above the factory—that's where Da Mei and I lived. Da Mei and I lay on the top beds of our bunks. We were tired, but we couldn't sleep. We tossed and turned. We imagined all sorts of things. We would never see China again. I would never see my son again. Who would take our bodies back to China? If no one came to take us back to China, we would spend eternity in a foreign country. I missed my family. If only I could see them all one more time before I died.

With no one to help us, no one to drive us to safety, no one but ourselves to comfort us this close to death and separation from our families, we resigned ourselves to our fate. We lay on our beds with our sneakers on, clutching our bags tightly, and we waited.

*****

Eventually, we fell asleep. I don't know how long we actually slept, but a noise outside woke us up. I thought I was dreaming, but when I looked out the window, I could see it was already morning. I got up quickly and went outside.

People were coming back. The girls in our room returned. Their faces were tired and their eyes were red. They hadn't slept.

I ran to the phone store to make a call. This time my father picked up the phone.

"I'm okay, papa! The tsunami didn't come! We're all safe!"

"Thank heaven and earth! Thank you, Buddha!" he shouted.

He was overjoyed. I heard him tell my mother the news.

"I have to go back to work now, papa" I told him. "I will call you next time."

I went back to the barracks, brushed my teeth, and went to work, just like any other day. Back at the factory, people were standing around, sitting, and others were lying down tired from the ordeal. They were all discussing what we had all just been through, and sharing what they saw and what they heard.

We heard, for example, that when news of the Tsunami first broke, L&T factory had used their buses to take their workers to the airport to leave the island! Many others had the same idea.

It had been a rare sight. The road to the airport was packed with cars. The airport was jam-packed. In China we say it was *people mountain, people sea*–in other words, a mountain of people, a sea of people. There were locals, Chinese, Koreans, Japanese, Americans—people from the different countries living and working on Saipan all trying to get away. Those who couldn't leave headed to Mount Tapochau—the highest point on the island.

We heard that taxi drivers had been charging $20 and $30 to drive people to the airport or to the mountain. People were parked at the top and along the winding road leading to the peak.

From then on, even though the danger had passed, people's hearts were still restless. For many, the fear of being washed out to sea while living on a tiny island in the middle of the Pacific Ocean created a constant state of anxiety. Many contract workers wrote letters requesting to be sent back to China. In Mirage, about fifty people requested to be sent home. At L&T, at least 200 people requested and were sent back home.

The experience made me realize just how valuable life is.

After the danger had passed, I finally called my husband.

"Come back to China," he pleaded. "It's too dangerous."

"I want to make more money," I told him. "I don't want to come back now."

I had survived the Saipan Tsunami scare of 2000. I had to look forward. I would not stop until I reached the Yellow River.

*****

One day we heard that Atu, our big monitor, was going to China for a few weeks. Everyone was giving her money.

My friends said, "If you don't give her the money, she may make trouble for you when she comes back."

Da Mei and I each put one hundred dollars. And we took the money to Atu at her barracks. When she took the money, she looked at it with disgust. She obviously felt it was not enough. Everybody else was giving her $500, but we didn't care.

The Nightmare Ends, for Now...

Finally, in August of 2001, my friends and I decided to quit our jobs at Mirage. Da Mei, Gian Yin and I went to the Saipan Department of Labor and filed a case reporting the conditions of the barracks, the director and monitor's bribery schemes, and that they weren't paying us for the time we spent at home preparing our tickets. However, the labor department was too slow to take action. After two months of waiting, we went to the *federal* labor office. They quickly opened a case, and gave us TWA (Transitional Work Authorization) status, so we could look for work.

When Mirage found out that we had gone to open a case against them, they tried to intimidate us. Da Mei, and Gian Yin and I had already left the barracks and were renting a room together in Garapan, but our friends who were still working at Mirage told us the boss wanted to see us.

We went to the factory for a meeting. They offered to give each of us $1,000 to close the case. The Mirage boss knew he would lose the case if it went to court, and if he lost, he would have to pay *everybody* overtime. The US Labor worker told the manager, "you should pay everybody because you are wrong." After a few days, we got a message from Mirage telling us to come in to get a check. However, when we found out how much the check was for, we didn't go. It wouldn't cover all the overtime we were owed.

Then something strange happened. People told us that the manager at Mirage gave some money to the US Labor worker—a bribe—to make the case "go away."

The truth is, even if they hadn't told us, we knew something had happened, because the first time we went to talk to her, the labor representative treated us well and was very helpful. But, the next time we went to talk to her, just a few weeks later, she was very mean and treated us badly, so we knew that something had happened to change her heart.

Eventually, however, Mirage agreed to pay compensation to everyone at the factory. The amount each girl got paid was based on how long they were with the company. You got $120 if you were with the company one year; $200 if you were with the company two years; $300 if you were there three or more years.

Da Mei, Gian Yin and I didn't take the checks. If we counted the actual overtime we worked over those years, that settlement was not enough. Still, many people were happy, and everybody took the checks, except us.

The US Labor representative told me, "If you don't like the settlement, you can go and hire a lawyer." So that's what I did.

In China, we say *if you work at it hard enough, you can grind an iron into a needle.* We were persistent. We had gone to Saipan Labor, but they were too slow. We then went to US Labor. They gave us the TWA, but eventually got bribed by Mirage. This was our third attempt to get the justice we felt we deserved.

The lawyer who helped us open our third case against Mirage was an American woman named Pam.

When Mirage found out we opened a third case, they again sent a man from the office to offer us a compromise to settle out of court. He met us at our apartment in the San Jose hotel one morning at about 9:00 a.m., and talked to us for about half-hour.

This time, they wanted to pay us each $2,000 to close the case, but they wanted us to close the case first, then they would give us the money. We didn't trust him, or Mirage, and we told him so. So, he suggested that if we withdrew from the case one person at a time, they would give each person $700 until the entire case was withdrawn, and then we would get the remaining $1,300. We still didn't trust him, nor did we believe we would ever get our money, so we told him no, and he left.

We also knew if we closed the case, our TWA status would expire, and we would have thirty days to find a new job. If we couldn't find a job, we would have to leave Saipan. So, we decided to keep the case open while we looked for work.

Chapter 5: Marianas Fashion ▲

November 2001 to January 2002

While our labor case was pending, Da Mei, Giang Ying and I went out looking for jobs. At that time, it was very hard to find a factory job on Saipan. We went to many of the factories, but no one wanted to hire us. Factories didn't like hiring TWA workers because they thought we were troublemakers since we had court cases. They feared we would open a case against their factory, as well. We went to six factories and had no luck.

Then we went to Marianas Fashion, in San Antonio. I remember it was a Friday in November 2001. We went to the office that afternoon, and they told us to sit and wait for another woman—one of the office workers—to get back. We waited for about an hour. When the woman came, she asked us what machines we knew how to work. Everybody answered. She then took us inside the factory to take the test.

We were all nervous that we wouldn't pass. The test lasted for half-hour. The woman then came to us and said, "You can go out, now." We weren't sure if that meant we had passed or failed.

She had a book in her hand. I saw that our names were written in the book. As we were leaving, I saw her write something in the book, but I couldn't see what it was.

The three of us went back to the office and waited. We could see her talking to the other office workers, but since it was far from where we were sitting, we couldn't hear what was being said.

After about ten minutes, she came back to us and said, "The factory would like to hire you. You have to get us your identification and TWA information by tomorrow."

When we heard "hire you," you can't believe how happy we were, but we had to control ourselves. We couldn't let people in the office see our excitement! We hadn't worked in two months.

That afternoon, to celebrate, we spent ten dollars on fish, meat, some vegetables and soft drinks and took them home. In about an hour, we had dinner on the table. That night, we had a wonderful time and a good night's sleep. The next morning, we got up early, had breakfast, and went back to Marianas Fashion.

We waited outside the gate for about half hour with all the girls arriving for work. They looked at us very strange as we stood there with them, since we were all new. After about twenty minutes, the door to the factory opened and all the girls went inside. We couldn't go in as we didn't have ID cards. We had to wait for the boss, or an office worker to let us in.

When the office worker arrived, she told us to go to the office to hand in our papers, and then she took us inside the factory.

There were four lines of girls (A, B, C and D) working at sewing machines. However, she walked us past them to the packing department, and then she called the packing monitor. It was very busy at that time, and they needed more packers than sewing machine operators. When it wasn't as busy, she told us, they would have us working on the sewing machines.

My job was to put plastic on the clothes—mostly women's blouses. Giang's job was folding the clothes. The rolls of plastic were hung from above, so we had to work standing up. After a half-day's work, my legs were stiff and swollen in pain. My arms were aching terribly. We were accustomed to sitting and sewing all day. Standing and working pulling plastic sheets from rolls hanging above us was very new, very different and very uncomfortable.

That first day, we worked from 8:00 a.m. until 12:30 a.m. the next morning. Sixteen-and-a-half hours of straight standing! At the end of the day, I couldn't feel my legs to walk.

We went back home exhausted and in pain! We were too tired to eat. We simply showered and went to bed. When we lay down on the bed, we tossed and turned trying to find a way to rest without hurting our legs. The next morning, our legs were still sore.

When I thought about spending another full day standing, I was afraid to go, but we had no choice. We had to work.

Once back at the factory, Da Mei and I did nothing but complain. "My arm hurts. My leg hurts," we whined to each other. Giang was older than us. She didn't complain as much.

After three days, I really could not walk right. Da Mei, Giang and I talked about it.

"I don't want to stay here," I said.

"If you quit, you'll just stay in the house...and do what?" Giang asked. "Maybe tomorrow, we'll finish and get to work on the sewing machines," she added encouragingly.

Every day we hoped, but we ended up working in packing for almost an entire month. Some days, I actually cried from the pain. I tried to ease the pain by placing a cushion on the floor to stand on. It didn't help. After five minutes, the pain was the same.

That one month at Marianas Fashion felt like a whole year. My legs were swelling more and more. Da Mei and I finally decided that we couldn't take it anymore. We wanted to get out, but we didn't have any idea where we could go.

Da Mei had a friend who we asked for help. His name was Lance. He lived across the floor from us in the same hotel. He was from Sri Lanka, and worked at a Korean Factory as a security guard. So we asked him if he would talk to his boss to see if we could get a job there. He said he would try, but he was sure we would have to pay the manager at least $1,000 for the job.

We asked Giang if she wanted to leave with us. She said no. She didn't want to pay the $1,000. She was willing to stay at Marianas Fashion for a year to see how things went. She was already thinking of going back to China to take care of her son.

Meanwhile, Lance told my friend, John who was also from Sri Lanka, to tell me to tell Da Mei that he liked her, and that he would help us if he got a girlfriend out of the deal! We thought that was very funny.

When I told Da Mei, she laughed, "Tell him to help us first!" she said. Da Mei didn't have a boyfriend, so we decided to use her as our leverage to get Lance's help. If they got together as boyfriend and girlfriend, that might help us get a new job faster. Still, we ended up waiting for another month.

The rest of the time at Marianas Fashion was hell. There was a lot of pressure. Because we lived outside the barracks, and didn't have a car, it was very hard for us to get to work. Once we got to work, the monitors watched us like hawks. In addition, we never received a legitimate contract to work at Marianas Fashion.

We were actually working there illegally. There were many girls who had been there for many months without a valid contract.

If the boss learned that the labor department was coming to inspect the factory, they would tell the TWA girls like us not to come to work that day. It was very stressful. That's why I wanted so much to leave.

*****

Eventually, Lance told us he had made arrangements for us to see the manager. So, a few days later, we went to the manager's house, but she couldn't help us. She told us to see a Korean woman named Miss Kim, who was the girlfriend of the factory owner.

So, on a Sunday night in January 2002, Da Mei, Lance and I went to Miss Kim's house.

Just as Lance had said, Miss Kim wanted us each to pay her $1,000 to get us a job. We thought that was too much. We knew others were paying only $500. The price was $1,000 for us because we were TWA. She knew we were more desperate because nobody liked to hire TWA workers.

We thought about our options. As factory girls, we would have to work more than a month just to earn $1,000. But, we wanted to have a job, so we decided to pay her. She reminded us, of course, that we couldn't tell anybody. The money was paid and it was agreed that the next Monday, we would start our new jobs at Advanced Textiles, a factory in Navy Hill.

Gian Ying eventually found another job, too, but soon after she went back to China, as planned, to take care of her family.

Chapter 6: Advanced Textiles ▲

January 2002 to March 2003

So, the Monday morning after our meeting with Miss Kim, Da Mei and I waited outside Advanced Textiles factory for her to show up. At about 7:15a.m., she arrived, took us inside to get our time cards, and then showed us which line we would be working.

She assigned me to Line 3. Da Mei would be working on Line 1. Every line had about thirty girls.

Old Turtle Arrives

My big monitor at Advanced was named Gi. She was from China, Ling Buo. After a few days, however, Gi left, returned to China, and was replaced by another woman. I can't remember the new woman's name, because we always just called her "old turtle" from day one.

Old Turtle was from China, Ning Bo. She had a short haircut, a short neck and was very short and plump. Some of her teeth were missing. She was ill-shaped and looked deformed. She had a black heart and was cruel. She was stern and cold, prone to false displays of affection, and like many of the big monitors in garment factories, loved money as much as life.

She brought five girls with her from her previous factory. She took $500 from each girl to give her a job at Advanced. The boss liked her, but we knew she was two-faced. She acted one way in the office, and one way with us.

In China we say *fame portends trouble for men just as it does for pigs*. Everybody knew Old Turtle's reputation. She was very caustic and arbitrary. She liked to meddle in other people's business and cause trouble. She was also a compulsive liar.

She was our big monitor as well as the factory director. I remember when she came the first day. She looked at the floor of workers like a general surveying his troops.

After the first day, we got overtime. Sometimes we worked as many as fifteen hours a day.

On Saipan, the factories were either Hong Kong or Korean-owned. While Mirage had been a Hong Kong factory, Advanced Textiles was Korean-owned. They each had different styles and ways of operating. Hong Kong companies would usually check on the workers' quotas once for the day. Korean companies, however, checked your quota every hour. If you did not meet that hour's quota, the boss would get angry and scold you. So every hour of every day we were nervous about being scolded.

The time would never be enough to make the quota. To have any chance of meeting it, you could not take a break, or go to the bathroom, or even stop to drink water. If we fell behind, we used our lunch hours to catch up, or fix the garments that were done incorrectly. It was a lot of pressure every day.

A factory worker has to sit all day. Sometimes, we had to sit fifteen or sixteen hours every day. The circulation in our legs would get cut off. When we finished, our legs and feet would swell and look like stumps. We couldn't feel them. Our bottoms would look like we had urinated on ourselves; they would be so wet with sweat.

As a result of working in the same position for so many hours, some girls developed hemorrhoids.

The work could also be very dangerous. Sometimes, we would work so fast that the needles would sew into our fingers.

One day, a girl named Xiao Zhu was working at her sewing machine, when she suddenly screamed out in pain. It startled everyone on the floor. A needle had been driven into her hand. It was very deep. We saw blood spurting out of her hand, and it would not stop. She kept screaming over and over, "The pain!"

You cannot imagine what it is like to have a sewing machine needle driven into your finger. In China we say, *the nerves of the fingers are linked to the heart*. We knew the pain was tremendous. And those needles are very hard to remove. The boss called the hospital and someone took her to be treated. She was absent from work for two days, without pay. When Xiao came back, her finger was a little better, but it took a lot of time for it to heal completely.

I remember another girl had a needle go completely through her fingertip and out the other side. She shouted and cried very loudly. We all stopped working to look and to help. Someone got some peroxide. Some one gave her a band-aid.

The band-aid was too small, and there was just too much blood. She also had to go to the hospital, where she stayed for about one hour, as the doctors treated her. Her case was very bad. Her finger got infected, and was draining pus every day. She was given antibiotics. Her finger was no good, but she had to keep coming to work or else she wouldn't get paid.

Sometimes the boss would see that her finger was bad and give her easier work to do. After about two months, her finger was healed to where she could go back to her regular work.

I also had something similar happen to me. While I was working, a pair of scissors fell off the table and sliced my ankle and cut open a vein. The blood kept coming. In a few minutes there was a puddle at my feet. I got scared. Even Old Turtle got scared. She went to the office and got the office workers to come to help. They gave me medicine, and applied bandages to try to stop the blood. After about half hour, the wound clotted and stopped bleeding. At that point, I didn't feel any pain, but the next day, my feet were tender and hurt when I walked.

This sort of thing happened very often to factory girls.

*****

However, there was one thing that happened to me that I'll never forget, that made me hate Old Turtle even more.

It happened in January 2003. At that time, the factory was very busy. We worked seventeen hours every day from 8:00 a.m. one day to 3:00 a.m. the next morning. Whenever we finished work that late, we would take a taxi home. Once home, we would have to cook lunch for the next day and shower. By the time we finished, it would be 5:00 a.m. or 6:00 a.m. By 7:00 a.m.—just two hours later —we had to get ready to work again. We had no time to sleep.

People are not made from iron. We are only human, and different people have different strengths and constitutions. My body was not as healthy. I was always feeling sick. Perhaps I had eaten something bad, or perhaps I was just too drained from working so hard, but my stomach started running. That day, I went to the bathroom seven times. I felt like I was dying. Unfortunately, the company was being pressured to finish production quickly.

My work was always very good. I'm very conscientious, but I'm shy to open my mouth to ask for time off. This time, however, my strength did not match my ambitions, and I talked to Old Turtle.

"My stomach is not good. I cannot work," I told her. "I just don't have the energy. I'd like to leave early."

"No, you cannot," she said. "If you go, who will do your work, hmmm?"

She was right. That job was one that only I could do.

Then, she said, "Maybe you just want to go home to sleep."

That made me very angry. She was accusing me of faking illness, pretending to be sick, just so I could go home. Old Turtle was as cruel and heartless as a wolf. I was in real misery.

"Why would I pretend? You think I like to be sick?" I asked.

It was very hard to believe she would actually say that to me, but I was *like a dumb person tasting bitter herbs*. I couldn't express what I was feeling, and there was no way I could convince her. I simply had to go back to work.

At about 11:00 p.m., I went to the bathroom again. When I got up to leave, I felt dizzy, and then everything went black. I don't know how long I was passed out on the bathroom floor. Eventually, another girl came in and found me. She called Old Turtle and another coworker, and they carried me to my workstation.

After a few minutes, I regained consciousness. I heard the other girls telling the monitor that I looked very bad, and that she should let me go home. Old Turtle had a look on her face that said she didn't want me to go home, but she now felt obligated. I felt like I wanted to cut her into a thousand pieces.

I went to the hospital, where they gave me an injection and some pills. Then, I went back home and slept all night. The next morning, I was still very tired, but I got up knowing that the factory had a big order to fill and needed my help. So I went to work.

When Old Turtle saw me that morning, she smiled and said, "Yesterday, you were so sick. How did you get well so quickly, hmmm?"

I could tell by the way she spoke that she still didn't believe that I was sick. She was hiding a dagger behind her smile.

In China, we describe people like that by saying *what can you expect from a dog but a bark*? Sometimes I cannot understand why people are so self-centered and inconsiderate. Why can't people be more compassionate? They only think about themselves and their own interests. They are not concerned about the safety and feelings of others. Old Turtle is someone I will never understand.

I remember there was a girl named Hong from Ning Bo. In September 2002, Hong arrived at the factory and joined the line I was working in, with Old Turtle as our monitor. She was plump and had pigtails in her hair. She was quite shy and introverted, and not very talkative. This was probably the reason for her bad fortune.

Almost from the day she arrived, Old Turtle, would use abusive language, and scold Hong every hour of every day.

"Why are you so slow?" she would yell at her. "Why are you so clumsy? Why did you come here? You should have stayed at home in China! What makes you think you belong here?"

With poor Hong, Old Turtle was always *looking for the worm in the egg*, something that wasn't there, something to find a fault with in her work, her productivity or just about anything.

Hong was a pitiful girl. Every day she would look so sad and dejected. She was a very hard worker, and she wanted to meet her quota and please Old Turtle. So, she didn't talk. We never saw her go to the bathroom. Over time, however, the work and mental pressure started to affect her. We saw her changing.

She didn't eat or sleep. Sometimes in the early morning, she would secretly go out onto the streets of Saipan. To feel safe, she even started sleeping with a big scissors under her pillow. It was obvious she was developing mental problems. We all noticed she was acting differently. Hong's friends told Old Turtle what was happening, but Old Turtle didn't listen to anybody. She still abused poor Hong and kept at her mercilessly. It was unbearable.

In China, if people see a rat crossing the street, everybody wants to hit it. Old Turtle was our rat.

And then, we noticed Hong didn't show up to work for three days. The first day, everybody thought she was just sick, so we didn't think anything was strange. By the second day, however, we realized she was not at the barracks either. We started to worry, wondering where she might be.

Even Old Turtle started to feel something bad had happened, and that she might be responsible.

Three days passed, and there was still no sign of Hong. Her friends went to the office, and told the boss she was missing, and how Old Turtle had been treating her. It caused quite a stir. The boss scolded Old Turtle for being so hard on Hong. Even he said it was not good to be so hostile to the workers.

What should we do? Everybody was worried about Hong.

And then, suddenly, after three days, Hong returned safely. Nobody knew where she had been, or how she had been living. We were genuinely concerned about her. We asked her all sorts of questions, but she didn't answer us, and never revealed any details.

The boss decided that for her health, and for the company's bottom line profits—he didn't want to pay for mental treatment—that he would send her back to China. He called her to his office.

"We know you've only been here two months," the boss told her, "but we cannot keep you here."

According to the contract we all signed in China, if you go back in less than three months, you can get half your fee back, but Hong didn't want to go back. She was from the country, and was very poor. She needed the money. But every day the boss would try to persuade her. Her friends, too, advised her to go back home for treatment. Eventually she agreed. A week later, Hong was gone.

It was very sad. Poor Hong didn't stay long enough to make any money, and she also lost money, since she would only get half her fee back. What's more, she returned home in worse mental condition than when she left. In China we say, *the hen has flown away and the eggs have been broken*. Everything was lost.

About a year later, after I had left Advanced, I heard that Hong came back to Saipan, and returned to work for Advanced, which, by that time had changed locations and was named Rifu.

Machine Man vs Monitor "Smack Down"

Even though I was now at a different factory, I still found reason to hate the machine men here too. They acted pretty much the same as they did at Mirage. At Advanced, however, we could ask the monitor to call the machine men to fix our machines. Most line monitors were women, but at Advanced, the line monitor for line #1 was a man from Shanghai. His name was Mr. Shen.

Once, Mr. Shen called the machine man to fix the machine for a girl on his line. He didn't come. So, Mr. Shen went back to ask him again. Machine Man told him to wait.

The machine man at Advanced was my line monitor's boyfriend. Whenever our monitor called him, he always responded right away. So, even though Mr. Shen had called him twice, when our monitor went to his office to call on him, he came running, close behind her, as she returned to the line.

He was so close behind her, in fact, that if she had suddenly stopped walking, he would have tripped over her!

When Mr. Shen saw this, he got angry.

After Machine Man fixed his girlfriend's worker's machine, he finally came to Mr. Shen's line to fix his worker's machine.

Mr. Shen, angry at the way he was being treated, started scolding Machine Man, who took offense at being scolded.

"If I don't want to fix your machine, what are you going to do?" Machine Man asked. "I decide whose machine I fix, not you!"

A fight was brewing. We all knew Machine Man didn't like Mr. Shen, because Machine man's girlfriend—our line monitor—didn't like Mr. Shen.

Mr. Shen always lied on his reports to get his line authorized for overtime. The director was always comparing the other line monitors (including Machine Man's girlfriend) to Mr. Shen, and telling them all to be more like him.

And then, it happened. Mr. Shen said something that really made Machine Man angry. Machine Man swung and hit Mr. Shen in the eye. Mr. Shen swung back and hit him in the face. Machine man jumped over the table and they started fighting. Clothes fell on the floor. People started cheering. Others were laughing at the scene.

The girls on my line wanted the Machine Man to win. His girlfriend was our line monitor, and he was good to our line. Plus, we didn't like Mr. Shen. For me, though, I still didn't like any machine man, not even one who was good to our line.

The girls on Mr. Shen's line were cheering for him. The other monitors tried to stop the fight, but couldn't. Then, someone ran to the office to get the director, a Korean woman named Ms. Jing, who came running, shouting at the top of her lungs.

"Stop! Stop!" she yelled.

She was breathless as she got to the scene.

"What happened?" she asked, in the little English she knew.

Both men were shouting their side of the story in Chinese to Ms. Jing. But she couldn't speak Chinese, and neither Mr. Shen nor Machine Man could speak Korean, and only Mr. Shen could speak English, but just a little. Ms. Jing took them both to the office, where a Chinese-Korean office worker, who could speak both Chinese and Korean, translated for everyone.

She scolded them and told them not to fight again. Everyone returned to work, but the drama wasn't over.

The fight had been on a Friday. On the following Monday, Machine Man came to work with a swollen black eye.

We were all curious to know what happened. We found out that Mr. Shen and Machine Man had met somewhere outside, away from the factory, by mutual agreement, to continue their fight! From the looks of Machine Man's eye and face, I think Mr. Shen won. Good. I hated machine men.

As I said before, from back at Mirage, I developed a dislike of the self-righteous machine men, so I hated them all. Even if he was good to our line, he was still mistreating the other girls and abusing his position. We're all foreigners in a strange land. We're all here for the same reason. No one should ever think they are better than another person.

Chapter 7: Rifu ▲

March 2003 to June 2003

The Ways of Rifu

By March of 2003, everyone at Advanced Textiles was moved to a new factory location in Dan Dan. The reason for the move, according to rumor, was that the new location was not charging rent. Before the move, our boss at Advanced started splitting up some of the lines in order to provide new workers to the boss at the new location, which was called Rifu.

However, conditions at Rifu were not good. The boss at the new location was very stingy. He didn't even like to buy water for the workers. He would walk around every day inspecting the lines. If he saw something he didn't like, he would scold us. We had to keep the floors spotless. If he saw you doing something he didn't like, he would make you punch out and go home right away. He wanted everybody to be busy. The machine men who fixed the machines had to be kept busy, too. So even if they didn't have machines to fix, they had to help the sewing machine operators with their work. We never saw him smile.

I'm happy and lucky that I wasn't in the first set of girls to go to the new company. I heard that it was so bad, that many girls, one by one, were asking for tickets to go back to China.

However, on the positive side, Rifu had many contracts to fill. They had overtime every day. We could work twelve to fourteen hours every day. If you had the energy and wanted to make money, Rifu was the place.

Escape From Rifu

Eventually, however, all of us moved to the new location. Shortly after Da Mei and I started to work at the new location, the boss came up with new rules. According to the new rules, we now had to live in the barracks and have a boarding cost and meal allowance deducted from our checks. If we didn't agree to this, then when our contracts expired, we would not be renewed.

We didn't want to live in the barracks. We had gotten used to living on our own after leaving Mirage. And, like most barracks, the food was no good, and the rooms were very noisy.

We weren't the only ones. Many people didn't want to live or eat in the barracks, but the boss didn't care. If we wanted to work at Rifu, we had to abide by his rules. Some girls even agreed to have the room and meal fee deducted, even though they didn't stay or eat there. I refused to do that. I decided it was time to leave.

I wanted to look for a new job, but at the same time I didn't want to go. It's funny. As bad as it was, I had been working at Advanced/Rifu for a year and a half, and had gotten used to it. When you stay in one place, you get to know the people, and the system. Even though we were unhappy, we knew the ways of Rifu. If we left, we would have to start from scratch with a new boss, new monitors and a new system. We thought hard about that.

Eventually, we went to the office and spoke to the director —a Chinese Korean lady named Gina—and told her we wanted to stay off site. If we could live off site, we would continue to work. If we could not live on our own, then we would quit.

She told us she would have to speak to the big boss—the owner—Mr. Joe. We knew our work was very good and we were fast workers. We knew the factory didn't want to lose good workers like us. Gina told us that Mr. Joe would give us an answer soon.

Da Mei and I waited for about one week, but didn't hear anything. So we visited Gina again. She told us that there was no answer from the owner. So we waited again for a few more days.

Then we went back again. This time we told her, "If you don't give us an answer, we will leave by tomorrow"

Then she told us, "The boss said you can live outside, but you have to eat in the barracks."

Da Mei and I weren't happy with that answer. Gina saw it.

"Mr. Joe is already being generous," she said. "The other girls aren't getting this opportunity, but your work is very good."

Da Mei and I didn't say anything. We went home, talked about it, and decided to leave Rifu. We decided we would walk out the next day.

The next day, we started work at 8:00 a.m. I was sitting at station 3, near the front of a line of about twenty-six girls. Da Mei was at the back of the line at about station 23. At 9:00 a.m., I got up and went to her station.

"Da Mei, let's go," I said.

She looked up nervously, and said, "Y-you want to leave now?" She was scared. Da Mei was always scared, but not me.

"Yes. I cannot stay here anymore. I don't even want to stay one more minute. Every time I see the director, I get mad. Makes me angry! Let's go!"

Da Mei and I took our little boxes of work items (a little cardboard box which included two sizes of scissors, tweezers, a little screwdriver, and a counter) and went to Old Turtle.When she realized what we were doing, Old Turtle spoke up.

"No, no, no. Don't leave now! If you leave now, nobody will do your job. I'll talk to the director. Can you stay for a while?" she asked pleadingly.

"No. I don't like waiting anymore," I said.

She got up from her station, and headed towards the office, as we took our little boxes and left.

When the security guard saw us, he asked us in English, "Why are you leaving?"

"I don't like working here," I replied.

The guard asked why.

"No reason. Just don't like."

Da Mei and I called for a taxi to take us to Hyunjin Factory in Gualo Rai. We hoped to make Hyunjin our new home.

Chapter 8: Hyunjin ▲

June 2003 to Feb 2005:

Hyunjin

A few days before we had walked out of Rifu, Da Mei and I had heard which companies had vacancies. We knew that Hyunjin was hiring.

So, in about five minutes, the taxi took us from Rifu, to Hyunjin factory. The Hyunjin office was upstairs. It was a small office, so small that when you went inside, you had to bend down. We walked into the office and talked to a worker there.

"Does your company have work?" I asked.

"Yes," she replied.

It didn't seem to matter that we were TWA. At that time, Hyunjin was open to hiring people who had open cases.

Hyunjin was also a Korean company, like Rifu. They had eight lines. Four lines were sewing coats. The other four lines sewed pants. From where we were in the office, we could see the factory floor, and the girls working very fast on the machines sewing the coats. Da Mei and I were impressed.

They asked us what machine we knew how to operate. Da Mei and I were very scared because we had never sewn winter clothes before. We knew the machines, but were not experienced at using them. We were afraid we wouldn't pass the test. Da Mei and I stayed in the office. After about five minutes, the office worker told us to go downstairs where there would be someone waiting for us.

We went downstairs and met a woman named Jing. She was tall and had a ponytail. She told me to report to Line 7 to take the test. They were sewing pants—which I was very good at—not winter coats. I was relieved.

She then pointed to the machine and said, "Work here."

I had used that brand of machine before, so it was no problem. After I worked for about half-hour, a woman named Hua came over to where I was working.

"You can go back to the office, now," she said.

My heart was beating quickly.

She then told me, "You passed. We'd like you to work here. When can you come to work? Can you start today?"

"No problem," I said.

"Come back to the office at one o'clock this afternoon," she said. "I'll give you your time card."

I was very lucky. Da Mei took the test on another line, and she, too, passed. That afternoon, we would both start working.

I returned to the Hyunjin office after lunch and received my time card. The office girl paged the Line 7 monitor to come to the office. Jing, who we had met before, appeared and took me to punch in. We learned that Jing was the agent for four of the lines, so she had four monitors reporting to her. She took me to Line 7 where I learned that Hua, would be my monitor. Hua reported to Jing. They were good friends. Hua was a small Chinese-Korean woman who was about 35 years old. I heard that she was quite easygoing. Jing told Hua that I would be working on her line. I could tell that both Jing and Hua were very kind-hearted. They seemed easy, understanding, reasonable and compassionate.

The only problem was that the factory floor was very hot. Because we were sewing winter clothes, we did a lot of ironing. There were not enough air conditioners to keep the floor cool, and some of the air conditioners were not working well. But I got a good feeling about working there.

A Very Different Experience

This company—Hyunjin—was the best I ever worked for. They had a good history and reputation. We felt very comfortable there. Everyone was friendly to each other. The boss, and the monitors all had good relationships. Everybody had enough time to go to the bathroom, to drink water, and coffee. Sometimes, we could even leave early if we had something personal to do.

Hyunjin's owner was a Korean man we simply called "the boss." Everybody said he was a good man. Everybody liked him. He was about 58 years old, short, simple and industrious. Every time he came to Saipan, he would wear the same clothes: simple dark blue slacks and a plaid shirt. Every time.

Every two months, he would make the trip from Korea to Saipan. Every time he came, he would gather the bosses and the monitors and treat them to dinner at a Korean restaurant.

During every visit, he would come to the factory and shake everyone's hand. He would visit each and every one of us girls on the lines, and talk to us. All the girls! Everybody. Every time.

"Are you tired? Is it good or not good working here?" he would ask. He would laugh with us and shake hands.

When people got sick, got headaches, or back pain, the boss would call the hospital, and even wait for us outside the factory to take us there. He never said no, not like the other factory bosses.

I think having a good boss makes you work hard and makes you feel like working. Even if the work is very hard, no matter. People like to have others praise them and give them understanding.

Hyunjin's boss had a daughter who died in America. It was his younger daughter, who had been living in either New York or California—I don't recall. She met in a car accident that took her life. He made a shrine for his daughter in the factory.

Every time he would visit, he would gaze sadly at a picture of himself and his daughter on the factory wall. He would stand there for several minutes just staring at the photograph. It was very sad. I heard that he named a museum in Korea after his daughter.

The boss gave encouragement rewards to very productive workers. Each month perhaps two people from each line would receive a $70 bonus. Lines would compete with each other. If a line exceeded their quota, the company gave the line $300 to use for parties on holidays like New Year's, Moon Day and Christmas.

Sometimes a line would get a tour of Saipan. New workers, who just arrived, would also get a tour of the island. Sometimes we would go out as a line to a restaurant, or have a barbecue.

The whole atmosphere at Hyunjin was very generous. I remember one day was Hua's birthday. Everybody gave $30, even the girls who typically didn't like to spend any money.

The monitors at Hyunjin were very nice. I remember one time I was sewing a pants pocket. Because the work was very hard, and I was careless, I made about 400 pockets with a mistake. I was very scared. I didn't want to tell Hua, but I was falling behind trying to correct them all. The other girl, who was waiting for my pants pockets to be finished, was getting impatient.

Hua heard that I was making mistakes and came to my station. She very calmly said, "Why do you make mistakes? You're always very careful. Why so careless this time?"

She wasn't scolding me. She also told another girl to come and help me unravel the pockets so that I could do them again.

I was very ashamed.

You fool. What's wrong with you? Why are you making mistakes? I asked as I scolded myself.

I don't know what happened that day. I don't know what was going on in my mind, but even after Hua spoke to me about it, I kept making the same mistake. Now I was scared. I was sure Hua would be very angry this time, scold me, or even send me home.

But surprisingly, she didn't. In fact, she made a joke of it!

"If you sew it wrong again, I'll hit you!" She said jokingly. This really affected me. I'll never forget how nice Hua was to me.

*****

At Hyunjin, whenever we had parties, everybody would get made up very beautifully. It was very different from work time. At work, we were all sweaty and untidy. At party time, we all looked like flowers competing with each other. We all got together, drinking, singing, dancing and laughing. The sounds of enjoyment made us all happy. It seemed we could swallow the whole world.

All of us at Hyunjin at that time understood we had come there from all over China—a vast territory with different cities. Every city was very far, and we understood we had only this one chance to know each other. We would cherish these friendships and our short time together. We all took many pictures. We wanted to have good memories for our lives.

Hell Beyond the Wall

But it wasn't all good times for everybody. Hyunjin had bad monitors, too. Da Mei and I were lucky to be assigned to sewing pants. However, there were four lines of girls on the other side of the factory who were working on the winter coats.

I soon discovered that the big monitor of those four lines was *mean like a tiger, and conniving like a shrew*. Line 7, where I worked, was next to the wall separating the two sides of the factory. Every day, we could hear the scolding from the other side.

Sometimes one monitor would be shouting, sometimes it was another. It never stopped. Sometimes the shouting was so loud we couldn't work, and we would all go to see what was happening.

The girls on the other side were being scolded like they were children. Many of the girls would cry from fear, embarrassment and shame. I don't think the monitors really thought about what they were doing. They didn't think about the girls' feelings. They would be especially mean to the new girls, and would scold them unmercifully, believing they would be too scared to talk back. It was a game to them. I know their type. In China, we say of them, *they bully the weak and fear the strong.*

I heard of one girl who had been there just one week, but got so nervous, and hated working there so much, that she asked for a ticket back to China.

Others would buy rings and jewelry and necklaces to bribe the monitors—hoping to be treated nicely. In the beginning, it might help you, but as you stayed longer, the monitor would eventually stop treating you special, and start scolding you again. Like hungry dogs, the monitors needed to be fed continuously. If you fed them with jewelry, it would keep them happy for a short time but, after a while, they would get hungry again.

Sometimes the monitors would try to bully the girls who had been there for a long time, but those girls weren't the small fish —they weren't *the weak.* One day, the Line 2 monitor and one of the older girls got into a fight, after the girl had answered her back defiantly. The shouting got louder. They started hitting each other and fought for ten minutes. The other girls tried to separate them. Their faces were bruised. Afterwards, the boss disciplined them both. But, as usual, the worker got the worse punishment.

On the other side of the wall, there were fights every day. The big loser was always the worker. The boss always disciplines the worker, more. He always takes the monitor's side of a dispute.

*****

There was a big monitor at Hyunjin—on the other side— who we called "fat woman." She was tall and fat. She was vicious and loved money very much. She managed four lines. She got the position because she was the manager's girlfriend.

The way it worked in a factory is that when a factory girl wanted to get her contract renewed, the boss would ask the big monitor for her recommendations. Since the big monitor worked with the girls every day, she knew which girls deserved to be renewed and which ones didn't. The big monitor, therefore, would have the final say, and the ultimate power over whether a worker's contract would be renewed or not.

Fat Woman was the type who would always lie whenever she passed on information. She would tell a girl who was up for renewal that the office didn't want to renew her, just to keep the girl guessing. She would also use this as a ploy to get money.

"The office has already decided," she would tell a girl. "But, if you want to renew, I can help you." She was hinting that she would help her to renew if she paid her money.

We all knew the game. Some girls desperately wanted the contract, so they would pay anywhere from $500 to $1000 to Fat Woman. If you didn't give her the money, she would make up a reason to tell the boss why you shouldn't be renewed—she would lie and say your work was no good, or that you weren't fast enough.

She would extort money like this from many girls. The floor monitors on the other side of the wall were all the same. It seemed that everybody was evil. Line 7—where I worked—and line 8 were a world apart from lines 1 through 6 on the other side of the wall. It was like two different factories. Nobody could believe things were so different just beyond the wall.

Pretty Flowers

The Line 2 monitor and the packing boss were also dating each other. The Line 3 monitor and the quality assurance boss were also together. All these women were monitors because their boyfriends had the positions and could help them. They always dressed very well, wore a lot of makeup, and reeked of perfume. They looked like cadavers.

The quality assurance boss was very ugly, but he was a playboy. He could always get many of the factory girls to be his girlfriends because he was Korean. You see, in China, in the cities near Korea, the girls worshiped the Koreans. Once some young girls found out that a person was Korean—man or woman—they would bow unctuously, and try to win their favor.

The girls in the Korean boss' office were there just like flowers in a vase—just for their beauty. They were all young and pretty, and mostly all virgins when they came to work there. Within a month or two they would still be young and pretty, but....

Typhoon!

One day, in March 2004, the radio and television news informed us there was a big typhoon headed for Saipan. Everybody was advised to take precautions in preparation. I remember that afternoon, I saw three factory maintenance men cover the windows with wood and strengthen the doors. By that evening, the rain started, and the wind started to blow. We were still at work.

We worked until 11:40 p.m. that night. By the time we finished, the storm was raging so hard that we could not go outside. The thunder sounded loudly. Lightning was flashing. We waited for a while, but things only got worse. John picked me up and we started towards home. The roads were flooded, and cars were inching their way along. We couldn't see through the windshield.

Once we got home, we discovered there was no electricity, and no water. By that time, the wind was getting even stronger. It was a high-pitched howl that sounded frighteningly like a baby crying. Trees were falling. It was impossible to sleep. The news report had said that the storm would hit full force in the morning at about five o'clock.

Early the next morning, police cars drove around checking on homes in our neighborhood to make sure everyone was safe.

At about 5:00 a.m., I got up and looked outside. The street was littered with coconut trees. Some houses had been damaged. However, what we had experienced was only a small storm. The big one was still to come. Even so, the area looked devastated. Everything was bleak.

That day, because there was no electricity, I felt there would be no work at the factory. However, I called Hyunjin just to make sure. One of the office workers answered the phone and told us we had to come to work first, and then the boss would decide whether we worked that day or not.

Driving to the factory was nearly impossible. There were trees everywhere, and the roads were full of potholes and water. There was mud and stones everywhere. What was usually a ten minute drive took us about thirty minutes.

Once at the factory, the security guard had us all wait outside the factory door until the office staff arrived. There were a few people outside discussing whether there was work that day or not. In a few minutes, one of the office workers came out and made an announcement.

"Today, you don't have to work," she told us. "There's no power, and CUC* cannot restore power in time."

They told everyone to go back home.

It was still raining. The wind was still roaring. It was strong enough to sweep any one of us off our feet. News reports said that by 2:00 a.m. the next morning, the full force of the typhoon would hit, and would pass later that morning.

Once I got home, I discovered the floor in my apartment was flooded, and rainwater had soaked my bed. I changed the sheets, moved the bed, and mopped up the floor. I was very hungry, but there was nothing to eat. In all the excitement, we hadn't had time to buy anything. Everything in the fridge had spoiled since there was no power. There were only a few packs of instant noodles.

With no power to run the water pump, there was also no water to shower. I used my washbowl to catch some rainwater outside my apartment, and took a quick bath. With no water, and no power, there was nothing to do. All I could do was lay on my bed and sleep. It reminded me of the helplessness I felt during the almost-Tsunami a few years before, but this was worse. The storm clouds made it very dark outside. There was no one on the streets. The wind made many different sounds and the thunder was terrifying.

In China, they tell young children that lightning can kill you —and that it often kills people who do bad things. I didn't think I would be punished for anything I had done, but seeing and hearing lightning and thunder like that always makes me feel like a frightened little girl.

The storm hit. All the howling, breaking, smashing, thunder and lightning lasted until 5:00 a.m., and then it passed.

*****

I left for work at 7:20 a.m. that morning and arrived at 7:40 a.m. When I got there, people were milling about talking about the typhoon. CUC had already restored power that morning, so we were able to start work at the factory on time at 8:00 a.m.

Shortly after we started sewing, I looked up and noticed that my friend, Shen Ju, wasn't at work.

"Why didn't Shen Ju come in?" I asked my friend, Zhang, who was behind me on line.

*CUC=Commonwealth Utilities Corporation

"I don't know," Zhang replied.

Usually, if someone is absent, we all knew why. We asked the monitor if she knew where Shen Ju was. We discovered she was at a school nearby and would arrive later.

Big Monitor told us that during the typhoon, a wall of Shen Ju's apartment had caved in and almost killed her. She and the other residents had been trapped under the rubble and had been hurt. We were all worried

By 10:00 a.m., Shen Ju arrived. Her eyes were red and wide. We could tell she hadn't slept and had been crying. We all cared about her. We asked what happened, and Shen Ju told us everything.

Shen Ju had rented a small house in Gualo Rai with six other people. A Filipino couple with two children had rented the house from a Chamorro family. The couple then rented a room inside to Shen Ju and another girl who worked on another line.

They were paying $60 each every month for a cheap house made from tin sheets. It was not very strong at all. When the winds picked up, the walls collapsed and trapped all six of them—four adults and two children. When the house fell down, they were hurt. Arms and legs were broken. Bodies were bruised and cut. They were helpless. They were sure they would die. They screamed for help for a long time—perhaps one or two hours, but no one could hear them over the sound of the typhoon.

After a long time, they heard the distant sound of sirens approaching. They decided that if they all shouted at the same time, that the combined sound might be heard. They used all their strength to shout "Help!" ten times. The police heard their voices, stopped their car, and started searching in the direction of the noise. When they saw the police officers arriving, everyone laughed and cried with relief.

When the two officers saw the condition of the house, they realized they couldn't rescue Shen Ju and the others by themselves. They radioed for assistance, and within a few minutes, more officers arrived and started pulling away the debris.

Inside, they were all shaking. They were drenched from the rain. They had cuts and bruises, and were soaked in blood. All the while, the wind and thunder was still going strong.

Shen Ju told us it took about an hour to rescue all of them. The police took them to a school in Chalan Kanoa that was being used as a temporary shelter.

When she arrived at the school, she saw people of all nationalities there. She stayed there all night, but it was too cold, and she was too shaken to sleep.

As she told us everything that happened, she cried. She had lost everything. She had no home, no food, and not even any dry clothes to change into, but she was lucky and happy to be alive. She asked for a day off to look for a new place to live.

She stayed with friends in the barracks for a week until she found a new place to live.

Many people lost much because of that typhoon—homes, food, and possessions. For three days there had been no power or water. We heard that the government was issuing relief tickets (it was either $70 or $75) for typhoon victims to use to buy food.

Mostly locals and Filipinos got their tickets, but the lines were very long. People waited for as much as a whole day to get their tickets. One of my Chinese coworkers said she waited for a whole half day, and still never made it to the front of the line. She gave up and went home. She never went back.

Many Chinese workers didn't collect their relief checks for a number of reasons. For many of us, the language barrier makes it difficult and intimidating to go through the process. Also, we just didn't have the time to spend a whole day waiting on line. We would have to take a taxi, wait on line all day—by the end of the day, our legs would be tired—we would have to buy food to eat, then take a taxi back. By the time it was all done, you might have $10 out of the $70 left! It wasn't worth it. In three days we could make that money from working on the line.

That was the first time I had ever experienced a typhoon. For contract workers, there is more than just the terror of the thunder and lightning. Being here during a natural disaster is a sad and lonely and terrifying experience, because you're far away from home with no support. If this had happened in China, it would have been different. There we have real friends and family. Here, there is no one to rely on. We only have ourselves. We can be there for each other as fellow Chinese, but in the end, we're all really still just strangers in a strange land working together in a factory.

"A Good Person is Always Safe and Well"

One of the big monitors at Hyunjin was named Jin. She was understanding and reasonable. In China we say, *a good person is always safe and well*. But what happened to Jin made me really doubt the truth of that saying.

Jin had gone back to China for vacation, and had not been back even two months, when she got a phone call at the factory office. It was her husband calling from China. We learned that Jin's youngest daughter had died in an accident. She had been about 11 or 12 years old.

Somebody had been driving a car, lost control and hit her daughter. When she heard the news she passed out. When she woke up, she couldn't believe it was happening. Just two months before, she and her daughter had been having such good times together. She loved both her children, but had a special adoration for her second daughter, and couldn't believe she was really gone.

To make matters worse, she couldn't go back to China for the funeral. She had just returned to Saipan. Tickets to China were expensive. There was also a lot of work to do at the factory.

For many weeks after, while at work, she would often just burst into tears. When we finished work, we would see her sitting outside alone crying. Many people tried to console her.

To survive, we knew she needed to be strong, but we knew how difficult it must be to lose a child. We could only imagine just how much pain she was in. When we looked at her, we felt her sadness. We wanted to help, but there was nothing we could do. Only time could help fade the memory and the pain.

Chapter 9: Return to China ▲

November 2004

How time flies. I came to Saipan on February 4, 2000. It was now November 2004, almost five years. My passport was only valid for five years of work, and could not be renewed from Saipan. That meant I had to go back to China to apply for a new one, so I needed to ask my boss for some time off.

Usually, when factory workers needed their passports renewed, the company they came to work for would help them renew, so there was never any need to go back to China. My situation, however, was different. I originally came to Saipan to work for Mirage, which was based in a different province in China than Hyunjin, where I now worked. It's difficult for a company in one province to renew a passport on behalf of someone from another province.

First I talked to the big monitor. She then asked the office manager. They told me that I could not go, because there was no one to replace me. In Hyunjin, everybody specialized in one task. But, I *had* to go, I thought to myself, if not, my passport would expire. I waited for a day, and then asked them again.

This time, the boss asked the monitors how my work was. The small monitor and the big monitor had a good impression of me. They liked my work. I was doing the work of two people. For this reason, the boss agreed to let me go home. They gave me only fifteen days. I told my big monitor that fifteen days might not be enough. I asked for five more days.

"Fifteen days is more than enough!" she said.

I didn't argue. I simply said I would try my best. She also told me that this factory generally never allowed girls to go back home to renew their passports.

Realizing that I would soon be home to see my parents and my son made me very happy. For days before I actually left, I couldn't eat or sleep. At night, I tossed and turned with excitement. The time moved like a snake walking. Each day felt like a year.

I worked until 5:00 p.m. on November 4, 2004. My flight—a non-stop to Shanghai—was on November 5, 2004 at 4:00 a.m. I was giddy with excitement. My thoughts were as turbulent as the sea. So many different things were running through my mind. I had been on Saipan for almost five years. My son was now seven years old. I wondered how he looked. Was he tall or short? Was he ugly or handsome? Was he fat or skinny? Maybe he wouldn't know me when he saw me. Would he call me mama?

And what about my parents? Were they healthy? Were they more wrinkled? I hoped they would be fine. They were my favorite persons in my life. I hoped they would be happy, as *immense as the east sea,* and live a long happy life.

November 5: Day 1 in China

The flight from Saipan to Shanghai was four hours, but I didn't feel like sleeping. From the moment we took off, I was already at Pudong Airport in my mind.

Soon, I heard the flight attendant's voice saying, "We've landed safely in Shanghai's Pudong airport."

When I first left to go to Saipan, I left from Hong Qiao airport. Hong Qiao was now used for domestic flights only. Pudong International Airport, where we had just landed, was very far from the city. I looked out the window. It was early in the morning—just about sunrise. The attendant, in a kind voice, told the passengers to be careful because the plane was still moving.

The sky was bright as we left the airplane. I walked out of the cabin into a cold breeze. There was a nip in the air. Everything was so different from Saipan. Being back in China was like being born again and returning to my mother's bosom. It felt so sweet.

I waited almost an hour to go through baggage check. Finally I got through, and my eyes searched the crowd for my son and my husband.

Suddenly, from behind the handrails, a little boy appeared and hugged me, and called me mommy. I looked at him. I could not believe this was my son! We had been separated for almost five years. He had changed so much. I had to search for a long time to see the familiar features I had left all those years ago.

He was not shy, either. He kept calling me mommy over and over. My heart started to break. I didn't know what I was feeling. For five years, I had never been able to give him a mother's love. I was not like other mothers who did their duty to their children. I felt so inadequate, and very ashamed.

As we sat in the car, he talked endlessly, asking me so many questions about Saipan.

"Was it nice? Was the work hard? How long will you stay in China?" He would not stop asking questions.

Eventually, though, as we drove the long drive home, he fell asleep. I looked at his beautiful face. I felt so content and proud of him. He was handsome. He was smart. He was my son.

As I looked out the taxi window, I realized that things were very different. It had been only five years, but everything had changed. Things were more thriving and prosperous now.

After about three hours of driving, we reached our city. I saw that everything there, too, had changed. Everything looked brand new with many high-rise buildings towering in the distance.

I carried my bags upstairs to our sixth floor apartment. Everything felt strange. It didn't feel like my house. My husband's parents were already waiting for us along with his brother's wife and son. When they saw me, with almost one voice they asked, "Why do you look so black and skinny?" I laughed nervously.

Earlier in the day, they went to the market to buy food—crab, shrimp—everything they knew I would like. My father-in-law had bought a box of grapes and oranges. I love grapes. I thought I would want to eat so many fruits when I got home, but when I saw the fruits, I couldn't eat them. I was reluctant. I don't know why. Maybe it was the cold weather.

By 11:00 a.m. that day, we had dinner. I had been away for five years without good food, real food. The food was warm and smelled great. It was prepared lovingly and made me feel so good.

After dinner, I walked to the mall where I found a sparkling array of beautiful things that made my eyes dizzy. I saw people spending a lot of money—it was almost as if they were getting things free. It was not like before. In China, people usually didn't like to buy things. They didn't like to spend the money.

I couldn't decide what I wanted to buy. I looked around for about four hours. Finally, I bought two pairs of shoes, a small suitcase, and a gift for my father—cigarettes and alcohol—along with healthy food for both my parents.

November 6th

The next morning, I rode the bus to visit my parents' house. It was about a five-hour bus ride to their house in Gian Hu.

My father was at the bus stop waiting for me. When I saw my father, I called to him, but he didn't recognize me. I had changed quite a bit in five years. My father didn't say anything at first. Then he asked, "Why are you so black, and so short and skinny?" When he looked at me, his eyes looked pained. He could tell I was not living a good life on Saipan.

I looked at my father. His hair was white. His face was wrinkled. I could not control myself. I started to cry. He hugged me, and wiped my tears away.

"Don't cry," he said. "Let's go home to see your mother."

I nodded. We walked the two miles home, talking cheerfully about everything under the sun.

Soon, from a distance, I could see my home. I saw a small form standing outside waiting for us. It was my mother. She was skinnier than when I left. She was also getting older. Her hair had just a little black color left.

I wanted them to know how much I missed them. When my mother saw me, she cried.

"You've finally come home," she said through her tears. "I miss you day and night."

I hugged her and cried. I wanted to tell her that everything was all right. I wanted to let her know about everything in Saipan, the good and the bad. I wanted to pour my heart out to her, but now, all I could do was cry.

We had a family dinner. My parents had prepared all my favorite foods. They kept filling my plate and telling me to eat. After dinner, we talked about Saipan, and my plans for the future.

Sunday, November 7th

Today, I rested.

Monday, November 8th,

The next day—Monday—my father and I went to get my new ID card. Because I had not been in China for a while, my card had expired. I also had to renew my passport. Unfortunately, that day was a holiday, so some of the workers at the ID office did not show up, and so it was busier than usual. We decided to leave.

However, my cousin had a friend who worked at the ID office. So we went to my cousin's house and asked if he could help us get things done quickly. My cousin came back to the ID office, and spoke with a man he knew there. With my cousin's friend's help, we were able to finish the renewal process in just half a day, but had to wait another two days to actually pick up the ID card.

Wednesday, November 10

On Wednesday, we went back to the ID office to pick up my ID card. Then we went to the Passport office.

I had fifteen days off from the factory, and already five days had passed. When we got to the passport renewal office, we explained my situation, and asked if I could get it done quickly.

The lady we spoke to told me that if I wanted it quickly, that I could take my forms directly to another office. It would cost ¥200, or about $25US, to renew the passport; much cheaper than on Saipan. On Saipan, it would have cost me $70 or $80US.

Fortunately, she didn't charge me extra for the faster service. She told my father to take the forms directly to another office in Nan Jing.

"How long do we have to wait?" I asked.

"Maybe one week," she replied. She was polite and kind. We finished our business, and then went back to my mother's house.

When I got back home, I called my best friend, Ling. I've known Ling since I was 20 years old. We could have heart-to-heart talks. We were like sisters. She's three years younger than I am. She also went to Saipan after I did, worked for about three years and then returned to China. At that time, she had worked at L&T factory, checking labels. Ling was short and skinny and weighed only about 85 lbs. If a typhoon came, it would surely take her away! She was very smart, and full of energy.

When we were on Saipan together, I would always visit her at her barracks. She would also come to visit me, and we would cook food together. On Saipan, so far from home, we didn't have many friends, but we had each other.

From the day she landed on Saipan, Ling had always wanted to go back to China. She had a boyfriend of seven years waiting for her. She always missed him, and wanted to get married and have children. She wanted to be a mother and wife. She said she was not young anymore, and could not wait. She said that once a woman was over 30, it was not good to have a baby. Ling was 29 when she left Saipan.

I knew Ling very well. She would make a dutiful wife and loving mother. She had a strong attachment to her family—that was important to her. In her immediate family, she was the oldest. She had two sisters and a younger brother in college. She gave the money she had earned from working in the factory to her brother for his college tuition.

I remember when she had decided to go home, we went to a pawnshop on Saipan to buy gifts for her boyfriend and her family. I bought two rings—one for her, and one for her boyfriend. She bought a ring for her father, and was eager to give it to him.

Sadly, however, Ling's father died while Ling had been on Saipan, but she never knew about it. Ling's mother didn't want to tell Ling that her father had died. She thought it would be too hard on her being so far away. She was scared that if she told Ling, she would be adding more hardships and misery to her life on Saipan, so she hid the truth. So, every time Ling called from Saipan and asked for her father, her mother would lie and tell her he was at work. Ling never suspected something was wrong.

Eventually, she told her mother she was returning to China to get married. When Ling's mother heard she was coming home, she knew, as we say in China, that *fire cannot be wrapped up in paper*, so she called Ling's boyfriend and asked him to tell Ling the bad news about her father when he picked her up from the airport.

Ling returned to China in August 2004. The night I went to the airport to see her off was very sad. She was my best friend, and I didn't want her to go home, but I knew her dreams. She was anxious to have her wedding day and move forward with her life.

I was also happy for her and her boyfriend. It was a seven-year love affair. She was practically already married. Their love was as deep as the sea. I was sorry I wouldn't be there for their wedding. Her boyfriend's house was very near to my husband's and my house.

I hoped that when she returned to China that she could help take care of my son. I asked, and she agreed.

The night she left I couldn't sleep. I felt such a deep loss. The next day, I bought a calling card and called her, and she told me about her father and what had happened. She couldn't believe it. She thought she was living a bad dream. She had loved her father very dearly, and was filled with regret that she never got to see him one last time before he died.

As she talked to me, she cried. I cried, too, and consoled her as best as I could, even though I knew she was devastated.

"Your father has already gone," I said. "He cannot come back. Try to look at the bright side of things."

"I bought him a ring," she cried. "*Now* who will I give it to?" she asked miserable and sad.

In China, if someone important like a parent dies, you cannot get married for at least twelve months. You can, of course, get married if you wish, but people will think you are being very disrespectful by not honoring the mourning period. So Ling waited to get married, but she and her boyfriend lived together.

To make the most of our time together—now that I was back in China—Ling came to stay with me and my mother and father. It was great to see her again. When I reunited with her, I discovered she had a son. She also got fat—like a small pig! She used to call *me* fat. Now she's fatter than me! She's about 55kilo (120 lbs.) No need to be scared of typhoons anymore, Ling!

While I was with my parents, my son called and asked me to come back to Wu Xi to be with him and his father. My mother also told me to go back to Wu Xi.

"Go home and stay with your son," she advised. "You have to cultivate the relationship with your son and husband."

It was not easy. I didn't want to be with my husband, but for my son, I would have to endure it.

Friday, November 12

My mother was right. I needed to be home to be with my son. I took the bus to go back to Wu Xi, and arrived at 7:00 p.m. I walked around for an hour, but I could not find my home! Things had changed so much, and I hadn't taken the trip by myself before. Eventually, after an hour of carrying my suitcase around, I had to call my husband to come and get me. When my husband and son heard I got lost, they laughed at me.

"Mommy, how could you get lost?" my son teased.

I explained that it was because it was at night. If it had been in the daytime, I told him, I'm sure I could have found it!

The next day, Ling came to Wu Xi to stay with the three of us—my husband, my son and me. We went to the market to buy lots of things for me to take back to Saipan.

I was busy every day. My brothers and sisters knew I was back in China, so they, too, wanted to come to visit and have dinner. The truth was, I was happy to have family and friends over. I really didn't want to spend time alone with my husband.

*****

My husband told me that since I was home every day, that I should drop my son off at school, and pick him up afterwards.

In China, the pressure on the students is tremendous. Children spend nine, sometimes ten hours at school. They have homework every day—a lot—even the first graders. If they don't finish, they have to stay at school to finish. My son was not doing well in school. I felt it was because of me. I was away on Saipan, and his father worked every day. There was no one to give him the support he needed, so his teachers kept him in school every day.

Wednesday, November 17

It was now twelve days into my trip. I would be going back to Saipan in just three days. Within four days of arriving, I had gotten my new passport. I was happy that the most important thing was now out of the way.

During the day, I often took my parents and son to the new park in the city. Every night, there were new events, and huge crowds of people and excitement. We took many, many pictures.

Every day, I went shopping for things I would need once I returned to Saipan. These days back in China were very precious. I was feeling the familiar love of my family. It was very nice. My son and I had some special interactions, but the coming separation was already causing him misery. When my son heard that I was soon to leave, he became very agitated.

"Can't you stay?" he begged. "Please don't go again."

My heart was broken. I could only say, "You're too young to understand. Mommy has to go make money to help you go to a good school. I'll be back again in another two years, OK?"

He nodded sadly.

November 22

November 22, 2004 was the day I was to fly back to Saipan. The round-trip ticket I had purchased from Saipan had no guarantee of a return seat, so I had to be at the airport early to go on standby.

That afternoon, we finished our last family dinner together, and then I took my suitcases downstairs in anticipation of the taxi ride. We told the driver—a friend of my husband's father—to be at our house at 1:00 p.m. The flight was scheduled for 8:00 p.m. that evening and it would take three hours to get to Pudong airport. We didn't want to be late.

We waited, and 1:00 p.m. came and went. I was anxious and angry, but what could I do? We called him many times. He kept telling us he was already on his way.

"Don't worry," he said. "We won't be late."

By 3:00 p.m. I felt like crying. I was sure I would miss the plane. The flight was scheduled to leave at 8:00 p.m. It would take us three hours to get to the airport.

At about 3:30 p.m. he showed up. Everyone was angry, but he still laughed and said, "Don't worry, we won't be late!"

I had a bad feeling. Perhaps life was playing a cruel joke on me. I hurriedly said goodbye to my family. My brother-in-law and my husband came with me.

We were driving as fast as we could on the highway. We were already having bad luck, and more was on the way. We discovered there was a terrible traffic jam between Wu Xi and Shu Zhou. There were cars on the road as far as the eye could see. That's when the taxi driver started to get upset. I was sitting in the car crying. But what could I do?

We couldn't do anything. We didn't move for twenty minutes. Many of the cars were trying to find other ways to get around the roadblock. We tried a different route. We would have to drive through Shu Zhou city. It was now already 5:00 p.m., and people were starting to get off work, which would only make things worse.

We didn't get past Shu Zhou city until after 6:00 p.m. When we finally got on the highway, he started driving at 80 m.p.h. I was scared. Everybody was scared. My heart was beating fast. My brother-in-law told him to slow down, but he said, "No problem, I know what I'm doing."

We got to Pudong Airport at 6:30 p.m. I rushed inside, checked my bags at the counter, and then asked about my flight.

"The plane is already full," the agent said to my disbelief. "We need two hours to check your bags. Now it's too late. You have to come early. I'll see if we can put you on the next flight."

Direct flights to Saipan were only on Mondays and Thursdays. The "next" flight was not for three more days. Today was already the fifteenth day off from my job at Hyunjin. I was worried about the boss, and my monitor. Maybe they would get angry. Maybe I would lose my job, but what could I do?

But things were not going to be as simple as putting me on another flight. The ticket agent told me that since my ticket was not purchased in China, that in order to change the return date, I would have to make arrangements directly with the company through which I purchased the tickets. That company was on Saipan. So, I bought a phone card and called my friend, John, on Saipan. I told him I could not come that night as originally planned, and that I would need his help to change the return date on the ticket. He told me to call him the next day while he went to the agent on Saipan and straightened things out. I hung up very upset.

Standing at the airport with all my bags and no flight, the four of us looked like we had just lost a battle. We were crestfallen. Now, we had to drive all the way back to Wu-Xi. We took my suitcases back to the car.

The rest of my family didn't know I missed the plane. When they discovered what had happened, they also got upset. The taxi driver—rightfully so—felt ashamed. He kept saying sorry over and over. He didn't know that airplane flights required you to come early. It wasn't like a bus, he thought, where people *without* tickets can get on and get your seat. He thought that as long as I had my ticket, that my seat would be reserved for me.

I didn't say anything on the drive back to Wu Xi. I was angry with my husband's father. He was the one who recommended that taxi driver. We spent money. We spent time. We wasted both.

Once back home, I lay on the bed all night depressed and restless. I could not sleep. I could not eat. I couldn't even drink a glass of water. I kept thinking that if people knew I missed my plane back to Saipan, they would laugh at me. People miss buses and trains, I thought, but missing a plane was embarrassing.

The next day, I went to the post office near my house to call my factory monitor to let her know what happened. I told her the next flight was not for three days. She didn't believe me.

"You just want to stay at home longer, don't you?" she asked. "You're making up stories and lying."

"No. Really. It's true," I said. I understood why she would think that, so I was not angry with her.

"Okay," she said. "Make sure you're not late again next time!"

Then I called John on Saipan to ask about the ticket. He said it would cost $100 to book a new flight. The next flight would be at the same time on the coming Thursday. I felt a little better.

In China, many people are superstitious. I am one of them. According to tradition, before going on my trip, I was supposed to go to a temple to burn incense for good luck. However, things had been so hectic, I didn't go. Was all of this Buddha's punishment for me? I don't know, but this time, I made a promise to go to the temple and do things the right way.

So, early Thursday morning, my husband and I rode our bicycles to the temple near our home. We bought candles and incense and prayed to Buddha for safety and protection on my trip, and to make the trip easy.

Afterwards, we went to a restaurant near the temple to have breakfast, and then went back home. My husband's father had taken my son to school while we were out, so I didn't get to give him a last goodbye kiss. I was very unhappy about that. He had wanted me to read him a story the night before, but I hadn't been able to. Tears rolled down my face when I thought about him.

My parents told me repeatedly that I should stay on Saipan no more than two more years. They said my son was getting older, and that I needed to be here for him. My mother knelt on the ground at my feet and cried. She begged me to promise her that I would return in two years. When I saw my mother crying, I felt the energy drain from my heart. I nodded, and said goodbye.

The flight was scheduled for Thursday at 8:00 p.m. This time we made different plans to get there. We would take the bus instead. We boarded the bus at 8:00 a.m. that morning. By 11:00 a.m., we arrived at Pudong Airport. Everything went smoothly. This time there would be no mistakes. We ate snacks, and waited.

John on Saipan told me someone would meet me at the airport with my ticket. At about 5:00 p.m., the man arrived, and I finally had my ticket in my hands. Only then did my heart stop racing, and did I start to relax.

At about 6:00 p.m., I checked in. There were a lot of people. By 7:00 p.m., I was in my seat on the plane.

At 8:00 p.m.—right on time—the plane pulled away from the gate. We took off, and I was finally on my way back to Saipan!

It was now November 25, 2004. At Hyunjin, we didn't work on Sundays. So, even though I had been in China for twenty-one days, it was actually my eighteenth day away from work.

*****

Sitting on the plane, I looked back, thought about big and little things, and sighed. Life was very hard.

Chapter 10: Return to Saipan ▲

November 2004

Back on Saipan

The flight from Shanghai to Saipan was about four hours. We landed at about 2:00 a.m. I had to wait a long time for our luggage, and to go through Customs and Immigration. As a result, I didn't leave the airport until 5:00 a.m.

I took a taxi back to my room in the Hyunjin barracks, prepared food for lunch, and by 7:00 a.m. I left to go to work.

When I arrived at the factory, my coworkers were very happy to see me. They asked me many questions about China, and about my family. When the big monitor and small monitor saw me, they didn't say anything. I thought they were angry with me, but soon they came and teased, "Why are you so black and skinny?"

I told them that while Saipan is peaceful and quiet, in China, I had many things to do. There, everything was not comfortable—the weather, family, responsibilities—these things made me upset and stressed all my weight away. They all laughed.

...and the Pretty Flowers Don't Bloom Forever

I returned to find the work as a Saipan factory girl just as stressful as when I left. I also returned to bad news. There was a rumor that Hyunjin factory would be cutting many jobs. Some said it would be closing. Some heard the big boss would be coming to Saipan next month to have a meeting, and that the factory would move to Vietnam, or a country where the expenses and salaries were lower than on Saipan. Every day there was a different story. This made us all distraught, and affected the quality of our work.

Everybody was worried. We didn't know what was true. They were all rumors, but in China we say, *there are no waves without wind.* We knew *something* was going to happen, but not what. We could only guess. We lived like this for several weeks.

Then, one afternoon, an announcement came over the loudspeaker. All the monitors were called into the office for a big meeting. The meeting lasted for two hours. We all felt this was the bad news we had been hoping against.

I had worked at three factories since being on Saipan— Mirage, Advanced-Rifu and now Hyunjin. This was, by far, the best one. Most everything was good. The big monitor and small monitors and coworkers were all generally pleasant. If it were true that the factory was closing, I would miss them all.

After the meeting, our small monitor came downstairs. From her face, everybody knew the news was not good. We all wanted to know the details, but we couldn't say anything during the day. It was difficult waiting. At the end of the day, we all went to the monitor's station to ask.

She confirmed the gossip. I really had hoped she would say it wasn't true, but she said yes, the factory would be closing. It wasn't considered appropriate for her to tell us workers the details of a meeting, so she couldn't say exactly when, but it was true.

From that day forward, everybody went to work a little sadder. Many of us started to look for new employers. About a week later, Big Boss from Korea did come to Saipan. At about 8:00 a.m. one day, he came onto the factory floor to speak to all of us.

"I and you my workers—as partners—have shared pleasure and pain for many years," he began. "I don't enjoy ending the partnership. I don't want to have to say goodbye. I like you all, but things have been changing...."

He went on to say, "If you wish to stay on Saipan, I will look for new employers for you. If you wish to go back to China, we will give you your ticket. I feel very sorry to give you all this bad news, but I have no way out because of business conditions, and I beg your forgiveness. Fees are getting too high, and salaries too, making it difficult to be profitable."

All the factories on Saipan had heard that the minimum wage would be increasing, so they wanted to get out early.*

After the meeting, everybody was upset. We all felt unhappy. We didn't want to accept the truth, but it was true. Nobody could change it. Hyunjin factory would soon be no more.

In China, we say *good times don't last long, and the pretty flowers don't bloom forever.*

My Friend, Zhang

Zhang Gui Rong is my best friend. She is from China, Yan Gie. Our friendship was very strong. We didn't keep secrets between us. We talked about everything. She is one year older than I am. I remember it was shortly after I first came to Hyunjin—perhaps two months—that she came to work on Saipan.

I remember when I first saw her, she looked very unhappy. She was tall and skinny and always looked upset. It seemed like she had lived an unlucky life, and had gone through many changes.

When we met, she told me she had been to Russia for one year. Then, after she returned to China, she took the test to come to Saipan. She worked behind me on the line in Hyunjin, so even during work time, we could whisper to each other.

For a long time, we talked and got to know each other. I learned that Zhang was a bit unsure and hesitant. She was also a very sentimental person. I also learned that my first impression of her was correct: life had not been lucky for her at all.

At twenty-one years of age, both her parents died at the same time in a highway accident. They had gone to visit another city in China, and their bus crashed. The death of her parents was a very big blow to her. Nobody can understand what that is like. It was a hard reality to accept.

Zhang was the oldest of three children. She had a younger brother and an even younger sister. After her parents died, she had to shoulder the family responsibilities and care for them both.

*This was in 2004. The first increase in the CNMI minimum wage from $3.05 to $3.55 would not take place until 2007.

Perhaps because she had lost her parents' love at an early age, it seemed Zhang got married in an effort to replace it, but she did not choose wisely. She and her husband did not have a good relationship. She once told me she realized her husband was not a good choice for her.

He was a liar who was always looking for other women. There were many times she knew he was with other women.

He was a violent man who even hit his own mother. Zhang and her husband had a daughter who was about six years old at the time we met. Zhang's husband hated her daughter. Zhang's mother-in-law told her that Zhang's husband would often hit their daughter, but he would warn the little girl not to tell anyone. Zhang learned the beatings were getting worse. And since her father had threatened her, Zhang's daughter never told Zhang about this. Every time she called China, her mother-in-law would tell her to come back home and arrange to let her take care of Zhang's daughter. Zhang's husband, however, didn't want that to happen.

He was also a leech. He would constantly demand money from Zhang since he knew she was earning a good salary on Saipan. They would always be fighting about money over the phone.

He was very contrary and unreasonable. Sometimes he would say yes, and then he would say no. I remember one time she went to China intending to get a divorce her husband had agreed to. When she got there, however, he changed his mind and refused to grant the divorce. Zhang couldn't do anything but return to Saipan.

While she was in China, however, she arranged to have her daughter cared for by some of her own family. However, after a few months, her husband located the child and took her back forcefully.

Zhang felt lonely on Saipan. She was always looking for a boyfriend to quell her loneliness. However, she was always choosing men just like her husband who were no good for her. They were either married, or simply mean. I couldn't understand why.

She once told me she had an interest in a Korean man who worked at a local supermarket called H-Mart. She knew he liked her as well. She said she liked him, but even I noticed that she always acted aloof and unreachable towards him. Every time she would go to the market to buy something, the Korean man would drop her home. He wanted to have the chance to get to know her.

She went there often—sometimes not buying anything at all —but simply "to look." They interacted like this for six months, and she never made it easy for him to start a relationship with her.

In China as well as Korea, August 15th is known as New Moon Night. A few days before, Zhang and the Korean man met at the supermarket. He had an offer and an ultimatum for her.

"I'm thinking about going back to Korea," he told her. "But if you want me to stay here on Saipan, I'll stay," he told Zhang. "If not, I'll go back to Korea. On New Moon Night, I'll wait for you at Memorial Park. If you meet me there I'll stay. If you don't show up, I'll know you don't want me."

I don't know what reason she had, but on New Moon Night, Zhang didn't go to meet him. He was left there waiting all alone. He gave up his hopes, and moved back to Korea.

Every day after that, Zhang would come to work with a sad face. She got even skinnier. She was lovesick, but it was too late. She had missed her opportunity.

I asked her why she never went to meet him that night. To this day, she can't tell me why. She doesn't know, but she immediately regretted not going to meet him, and hated herself for it. Every night, she would go out smoking and drinking with friends to drown the pain. For almost six months she punished and poisoned herself like this, but, over time, she slowly started to forget, forgive herself and move on.

The Party

To commemorate Hyunjin's closure, every line had a going-away party. My line's party was at a restaurant in San Antonio. I remember it was a Friday evening. The manager, the director, as well as the big monitor, and small monitor and everyone in our line were there. There were about thirty people in all—all Chinese.

At the beginning of the festivities, Big Monitor stood up and said, "Today, everybody has to drink! It doesn't matter if you drink or not, today you will!"

Zhang, and I didn't really drink, but the monitor gave us two glasses and insisted. It tasted like medicine! It felt like fire! We didn't like it at all! Zhang was the same as me. She could not hold liquor, but was a little better at it than I was. From that one shot, our faces got as red as apples. I'm sure we looked quite amusing.

Someone asked one of the waitresses for ice, and we put the ice down the backs of the manager and monitors and factory director! Everybody laughed! Soon, the floor was covered with ice and water. It was like a skating rink. Someone slipped and fell down, and everybody laughed again!

That night we were very happy. Everybody got drunk and was red in the face. We did Karaoke. We sang and danced. We felt young and carefree. It was a frenzied night of fun. We all wanted time to stand still.

We enjoyed ourselves until the restaurant closed at 5:00a.m! Afterwards, the factory director took us to *another* Korean restaurant! We had breakfast there until 6:30 in the morning. By then, we were all exhausted. We said our goodbyes and went back home. I slept all day Saturday.

I thought about that night for many weeks, and even today it makes me smile. But even then, as now, I also felt a strange sadness whenever I thought about it, because I knew nights like that would probably not happen again. Hyunjin would close, and we all would go our separate ways.

Forever Friends

As the final day at Hyunjin approached, our monitor asked us all to write our telephone numbers and addresses in China so we could all keep in touch wherever we ended up. She didn't want us to simply separate into the wind. She wanted us all to be able to keep in touch even after the factory closed. She made photocopies and gave everyone. I still have mine today. It was touching. She had given it much thought and it told us the experience of all of us working together at Hyunjin had really touched her too.

*****

As the boss had promised, he helped us find new jobs at other factories. He even took us to other companies to take the tests.

Zhang and I were lucky, however. We didn't have to go to another company to take a test. Another company had approached Hyunjin in search of workers, and we had the right experience. The new company was looking for workers who had experience making summer clothes. Even though Hyunjin's specialty was sewing *winter* clothes, Zhang and I had worked at Mirage and other factories where we worked on summer clothes, so we got the job.

Ever since learning that Hyunjin was closing, we were always worried about our next job. Now, with a promise of employment from this new company, we didn't have to worry anymore. It was a relief.

And what was the name of the new company we would be working? It was none other than Rifu. Yes, *without coincidences, there would be no stories.*

*****

With just a few days until the factory closed, some of the girls had already gone and were working at new jobs. However, the work at Hyunjin was not yet completely finished, so the boss decided he would release the remaining girls to Rifu a few at a time rather than all at once.

On January 23, 2005, someone from the office came and told Zhang and me we had to start working at Rifu the next day.

Chapter 11: Rifu, Again! ▲

January 24, 2005 to March 24, 2005

Back in the Fire

The next day, January 24, 2005, Zhang and I went to start working at Rifu. We were standing outside waiting for the office manager to arrive. At 8:30 a.m., she arrived. When I saw her, she gave me a mean look. Her eyes told me she was a deceptive and tricky person, a methodical plotter.

There were six of us arriving for the first time that morning. She told us we had to attend a meeting. It was there that she started to tell us the rules.

"When you come to this factory to work," she said, "you must live in the barracks."

When she first came to Hyunjin recruiting workers, she never told us we had to live in the barracks. Everyone was angry. We all felt deceived. I asked why she hadn't told us that originally.

"If you don't like it," she said, "I'll give you a choice. You can either live in the barracks or eat in the barracks dining hall."

At that time it was very hard to find work in the garment factories, and she knew that. I decided I would work there for a few days and see what it was like. Then, if I didn't like it, I would leave.

"Within a few days, I expect your work to be up to the same speed and quality as the other girls'," she continued. She gave us only three days to get up to speed.

She asked me what machine I knew to operate. I told her, and she assigned me to the "B" line to work, because that would be easy for me. For many of the other girls, it was very hard. They were not accustomed to working on winter clothes like I was.

Our new monitor was always scolding the girls. She was very loud. It seemed like she could not stop. It was terrible. After just one day, my mind was ready to explode. Even after I got home that day, I could hear her angry voice echoing in my ears.

After that one day, I decided I really didn't want to return, but I had to force myself to go. I had no choice.

The next day, I realized I had an important errand to run, so I went to work and requested a half-day off—a few hours to take care of it. Before I could even finish telling her my reason, the big monitor got angry and scolded me.

"You just started working one day, and already want a day off!? Who do you think you are?" she asked angrily.

"I understand your viewpoint," I told her, "but if I don't go today, I won't be able to go again."

She wanted to know my reasons.

"Today is the last day to register for English classes," I told her. "That's why I want a few hours off. I want to learn how to speak English."

She finally said it was okay, but I know she didn't really want to grant my request. At that time I really wanted to tell her, "I really don't want to work here! You think I cannot find another job?" But I controlled my emotions. After I walked through the factory door, I was so angry. I knew that day that Rifu was no good.

I went to Saipan's Northern Marianas College to register. Unfortunately, I wasn't able to finish the entire process that day, and would have to ask for more time off. It would be easier to simply stay away from work rather than to ask Big Monitor for permission again. She would want to kill me! So, I decided I wouldn't go into work the next day.

When I didn't show up at work, Big Monitor called me.

"Why didn't you come to work?" she asked.

I told her that I had to finish registering for English classes.

"When will you finish registration?" she asked.

"Today," I told her.

"Okay, if you finish today, can you come back to work tomorrow?" she asked.

I thought about it for a few moments, and then said, "Okay."

After she hung up the phone, I remembered that in a few days it would be Chinese New Year. I told myself that after the New Year, I would look for a new job.

When I went to work the next day, she came to my station. Her whole attitude was different. I think she realized how good my work was, and how productive I was.

Because of the New Year holiday, the factory boss decided to give everybody two oranges, a bottle of soda and a small loaf of bread. I took the gifts and went home. I stayed at home for a few days. Zhang and another girl, who were still at Hyunjin, called me and asked me what it was like at Rifu. I told them the truth—it was terrible. They got scared. They too, didn't want to go to Rifu.

*****

Right after Chinese New Year, I phoned Sam Kwang Factory in San Antonio and asked if they needed any workers. My friend Ying was also planning to quit Rifu. When she discovered that I, too, didn't want to work at Rifu, she suggested we go to the office together to get our files so we could look for work.

The Rifu office worker computed how much we were owed, and told us to come back after one week. He told us that our files were kept at Rifu's other location. Ying and I went to the other location, got our files, and then went to Sam Kwang to take the test. After we passed the test, the Sam Kwang big monitor asked me how many years I had been on Saipan. When she heard five years, she didn't want to hire me. Most girls left Saipan after three years, so she felt that I wouldn't be committed to staying more than another year at most. She asked if I could work at least two years.

"Yes, I can," I replied.

Ying and I both had to promise her we would be able to work for at least two more years. After she determined we were sincere, she decided to hire us.

But even though we were hired, she told us we had to wait. There were too many people already working in the factory, and so there were not enough machines available. We would have to wait until some of the workers went back to China before they could hire us. They asked for our phone numbers and addresses, and told us they would call when they needed us.

A month passed with us just sitting at home waiting for Sam Kwang to call. It was very boring. We went to Sam Kwang about three or more times to ask what was happening. They kept telling us to wait. We started to worry that perhaps they didn't really want us.

Maybe they had plans to hire other workers. So, Ying and I went to apply at Onwell Factory in Chalan Kanoa. We completed the forms putting ourselves on the waiting list, and waited for Onwell to call.

By strange coincidence, on the same day that Onwell called to have us take the test, Sam Kwang finally called to let us know we could start right away.We didn't know what to do. Ying and I thought about it for a whole half-day. Even though the name "sam kwang" in China was not lucky—it means *everything is finished,* or *all is spent or depleted with nothing left*—we decided to go with the sure thing. We decided to work at Sam Kwang.

Chapter 12: Adding Frost to Snow ▲

2004

As the years pass here on Saipan, I miss my family in China more and more. I've been away now for nine years. I want to go back to visit my parents and my son, but I cannot. If I told anyone the real reason why, however, they would find it hard to believe. The truth is, even though I've been here for many years working hard, I don't have enough money to go.

"Where's all those years' worth of money?" people would ask me. It doesn't make sense. I didn't gamble. I didn't drink. I had avoided the jewelry store scam, I kept my money in the bank, and I knew how to save it. Even now, when I think about it, and talk about it, my heart pains me. Sometimes I want to cry, but I know crying cannot help.

Maybe I was immature. Maybe I was a fool. Maybe my heart was too soft. Maybe I am just simple. Maybe I don't know the immensity of the universe, or the ways and wisdom of the world, but here's what happened.

In 2004, I was working at Hyunjin factory. One day, after I finished work, I went back home. My friend John asked me, "Do you want a green card?"

At that time, I didn't know what a green card was. The words didn't mean anything to me. "What is green card?" I asked.

After he explained, I began to understand a little better just how good it might be to have one, so I said yes.

He told me he had a friend, a masseuse, who knew a police officer named Martinez. He told me Martinez was from Mexico, but he was a US citizen now living on Saipan. He told me that if I paid the money, then in two years I could get a green card.

"How much money is it?" I asked him.

"Ten thousand," he told me.

"I don't know," I said hesitantly. "I don't like."

"You can trust him," John assured me. "He's a police officer. He knows how to get green cards."

My heart was wavering with doubt.

"Let me think about it," I said. "I'll give you answer by tomorrow."

The next evening, John again asked me what I had decided.

"Did you decide?" he asked. "Martinez wants to see you."

"I don't like," I said again.

"Why don't you just see him first?" John suggested.

I agreed, and so we went to Martinez' house. Since it was close to where I was living at the time in Chalan Kanoa, we got there in just a few minutes. When I entered the house, there was a strong smell of alcohol. It was so strong, I felt like I couldn't breathe. I wanted to go back home right away, and my body language must have revealed it.

"Just wait," John begged me. "He'll be out soon."

In two minutes, a short, fat man appeared from another room. His face and neck were red. I could tell he had been drinking. He was bald. He looked to be about 55 years old. My first impression was that he was a scoundrel, sly and shrewd. Just seeing him made me uneasy.

John and I were sitting at a table. From a drawer, Martinez took out some photographs to show us. It was a photo of a woman and some children he said were his wife and children. He told us his wife took the children to American when she got her green card.

Next, he showed us a picture of a Korean woman. He told us that he had helped her get her green card a few months before.

When Martinez talked about what happened, John got excited. He asked Martinez, how much it would cost.

"$12,000 US," Martinez replied.

"That's very expensive," John said. "Can you discount it?"

"Twelve thousand isn't expensive," he said. "If you don't want it, no problem. I have another person who is waiting for one who would gladly pay even more."

Even I could tell that was a trick to persuade us to act right away. Then he told us not to tell anyone what we were doing. He told us that if we told anyone, he would get in trouble and go to jail. I should really have left then.

We were there for about five minutes. When we stood to leave, he asked for a telephone number to contact us. John gave him a number to reach him, and we went back home.

"What do you think you want to do?" John asked, once we got home.

"If I had $12,000," I said, "I could go back to China and start my own business."

At that time, I had about $10,000 in my bank account. It would have been more, but I had already lent John about $13,000 over the course of three years for different things—to help his sister get married, to start a business, for his mother's illness—for many things. Whenever he asked me for money, I felt I was being mean if I didn't give it to him. Now, I was already waiting for him to pay me back. He had promised he would pay me back $500 every month. I thought that since I was waiting for him to pay me back, and would be on Saipan anyway, that perhaps it was a good idea to use the time to wait for a green card. However, I didn't want to give Martinez my money. I didn't trust him.

Three days later, Martinez called John. He had dropped his price to $8,000.

"Eight thousand," he said, "and in two years, you'll have a green card. You can give me half now, and when you get the green card, you can pay me the rest."

"This seems good," John reasoned. "Where else can you get a green card for $8,000? And he's a police officer. If you miss a chance like this, you might not get another."

I was so confused, but I had now become obsessed with the idea of getting a green card. I didn't know what to do.

In two years, I thought to myself, I could get a green card, and also get most of the money that John owed me. I agreed.

Three days later, John called to tell me Martinez needed $3,000 to start the process. We would meet at 12:30 p.m. the next day, at Oleai Restaurant, to give him the first payment of $1,500.

"If you give him the money, you have to get something in writing—some kind of receipt," I told John.

"Don't be scared," he told me. "Nothing bad will happen. Besides, he's a police officer."

John seemed convinced that Martinez was legitimate. I went to the bank during my lunch hour, withdrew $1,500, put it in an envelope, and we went to Oleai and waited.

At first I thought it was strange.

"Why did he tell us to wait here?" I asked John.

"He works here now," John said, "as a cook."

"You told me he's a policeman," I said, shocked. "Why is he working here at a restaurant now?"

"He had a little incident. He got into a fight, and the police chief suspended him as punishment," John said. "It was only temporary. Next month, he'll be back at the police station."

I didn't ask any more questions.

After a few minutes, Martinez, the "old wolf" appeared with sweat streaming down his back. He wanted to talk to John in private. They whispered to each other so I couldn't hear. He took the money and went back inside the restaurant.

The next day he called John to request the additional $1,500. John called me at work to tell me. I started to get more uncomfortable. I had already given this strange man $1,500 with no receipt, nothing to show.

"You have to give him the other $1,500," John told me. "If not, he won't do anything."

I had no choice. We met the next day, at the same time and place, and I gave him the other $1,500.

When I realized that I had just given away $3,000, I felt like my spirit left my body. I immediately regretted it. A few days later, I told John I wanted my money back.

While I was at work in the factory, John went to the restaurant and asked Martinez for my money. Martinez refused, and promised that he would definitely get me my green card. Martinez told John he had already spent the money. He had used it, he said, to pay some debts, as he owed money to many different people.

I asked him for my money many times, but I knew it was too late. Even then, I knew I would never get my money back. I had been swindled. I had brought this darkness on myself. Three thousand dollars is about a half-year's salary for me. I am a factory worker. That money was my toil and sweat. In effect, I had wasted my energy all those months working for Martinez.

Two months later, Martinez surfaced again to ask for more money. He told John that he was going back to work on the police force, and he needed $50 for his medical exam, and $100 for his uniform. When John asked me for this, I wanted to slap him.

"I told you I wanted my money back from him!" I shouted. "Why are you coming to me now for more money? If you want, you can give him your money, but don't ask me for mine!"

He looked at me fiercely, and walked away. He later told me that he did, in fact, give $200 to Martinez.

We went to the police station twice to search for Martinez, and paged him from the front desk, but he never appeared.

Once, while we were driving, I spotted him in a car driving south on Beach Road. We followed him to a small store near the Chalan Kanoa post office. John approached him and again asked for my money. They started arguing and cursing at each other.

"If you don't like it, you can go to court!" Martinez finally shouted at John. He knew very well we could not go to court with this. And even if we could, John thought he might also lose his own job as a result of dealing with Martinez.

I heard later that Martinez swindled a local Chamorro woman out of her money. I heard that *she* had, in fact, taken him to court, but I don't know what ever happened with the case.

Martinez is a swindler, a liar and a drunk who would drink ten cans of beer at one time. He had a black heart. John once told me that Martinez wanted me to live with him. He told John if I would agree to live with him, he would fix the papers to get my green card, even though he knew John and I were together!

Maybe I'm a child, easy to dupe. Perhaps I just have bad luck. Maybe I am too naive, or too kind. I always want to help other people. That's my curse. Sometimes it seems that bad luck always flows like the sea to me. Hardly has one wave of bad luck subsided, when another washes into my life.

In another example of my bad luck, my brother's wife wanted to come to Saipan to work. John had a Korean friend who was the boss at La Mode, Inc., another factory on Saipan. I asked John to help get my sister-in-law a job, and that I would pay John's Korean friend $2,000 to hire her. John agreed to ask.

First, Korean Man told me to bring my sister-in-law's information, and copies of her credentials and identification. So I spoke to my sister-in-law and asked her to send me the information. I also told her about the $2,000 fee. She asked me to pay it first, and when she came to work on Saipan, she would pay me back.

Two months later, I received her information by mail. I then gave $2,000 to John to give to Korean Man. We waited for about four months, and never received any information. So, I asked John to go to La Mode to see what was happening. Korean Man told John that we needed to be patient.

After almost five months, there was still no news. Then, one day, while I was at work, a co-worker told me he heard that La Mode was closing. When I heard the news, I was *like a bird startled by the twang of a bowstring.* I was in a panic. For a long time, I couldn't speak. I didn't want to believe it. I hoped the news wasn't true. That evening, I went home and asked John to go to La Mode and find out if what I heard was true. That night I couldn't sleep.

The next day, John went to La Mode. It was just as I had heard and feared. La Mode factory was, in fact, closing.

I asked John to get my money back. Korean Man told John he would return my money, but he kept delaying. John and I went there many times to get my money, and he would always say next week, next month, or next time.

Four months earlier, after I told her things were in process, my sister-in-law, excited about coming to Saipan, quit her job and started to purchase things in preparation. Now, with La Mode closing, she had no job on Saipan, and no job in China either.

Later, after La Mode closed, Korean Man was still on Saipan. I learned he had his own small factory—employing five people. They worked many hours for him, but he never paid them. He would always say, next week, next month, or next time.

It's been almost four years. Even today, as I write this, I haven't ever gotten even one dollar back. I learned he owed many people money, and has since run back to Korea.

Sometimes I sit alone looking at the stars in the night sky and cry. I cannot remember how many times I've been scared to tell my parents. I'm afraid that they'll lose respect for me. Whenever I call, they ask me to come back to China, but I have a good reason to evade them. They always taught me never to lend money to people. I didn't listen, and now I am paying the price.

I am their only daughter. In China, filial piety—a love and respect for one's parents and ancestors—is very important. My parents want and expect me to take care of them as they get older.

After every phone call, I always feel very depressed. But no one knows all the difficulties I've had.

Once, I confided in my brother and told him what had happened to all of my money. I told him not to tell my parents. He promised to keep it a secret, but a month later, he broke his promise, and told my parents everything.

When I called my parents, they asked me about my money situation. They asked me how much I had lent to other people. I didn't tell them how much. If I told them exactly how much it was, they would have been very, very unhappy.

"I told you never to lend money to people," my father said. "You don't listen. Where are these men? When are they going to give you your money back?" he asked of John, Martinez, and Korean Man.

"They are here on Saipan," I told him. "I don't know when."

I knew I might not ever get the money back, but I lied to my parents to make them feel better. If they knew that I would never get the money back, they would get very angry.

They scolded me for a long time. They could tell I wanted to cry. When they realized that I was near tears, they calmed down. They didn't continue because they knew that what's done cannot be undone. If they complained too much, they knew it would make me even more depressed.

Two weeks later, my brother called. I was angry with him for betraying me.

"I told you not to tell them," I scolded. "I don't want them to worry about me."

"Next time, don't lend money," he said. "People lie. You can't believe everybody."

I promised him that I had learned my lesson and that I would not lend money any more. But I know in my heart that if someone I know and like asks me to help them, I cannot say no. Even before I had come to Saipan, one of my cousin-sisters had told me not to make the mistake of lending people money. She knew my heart, and that I always helped people in trouble.

Little by little, over the years and because of my trusting and kindness, I have lost most of my money. In all the years I worked, and all the money I earned, I accomplished nothing. In China, we would say, I *added frost to snow*. Adding frost to snow is "engaging in a futile, meaningless action that adds no visible benefit." That's what all my years of work on Saipan have been.

Where is Saipan?

Saipan is located in the western Pacific Ocean in a region of the world known as Micronesia. It's a short flight from Guam, 3 hours from Japan, and 4 hours from China. It is the capital of the US Commonwealth of the Northern Mariana Islands (CNMI), a popular tourist destination rich in history and culture.

Saipan, just 5 miles wide by 12 miles long, is the largest and most populated of the 14 islands making up the Northern Mariana Islands, an archipelago that stretches 400 miles (north to south) along the edge of the Marianas Trench (The deepest part of the earth's oceans).

As a result of a unique covenant with the United States, which took over administration of the islands after World War II, the CNMI controls its own immigration.

Garment factories were first established in the 1980s. Workers from China, Thailand, the Philippines, and other Micronesian islands, migrate to Saipan (and the neighboring islands of Tinian and Rota), to work for wages in US currency.

Me in China; three weeks after my wedding. (1996)

*Ling, Da Mei, me and Zhu Yan; Chinese New Year, Tinian;
I'm so fat! (2001)*

The final Hyunjin Party. It was a special place to work. (2004)

Zhang and me (Hyunjin, 2004)

Me and friends (Hyunjin, 2004)

Hua (My line monitor), Jing (Big Monitor) and me. Jing's daughter died while she was working on Saipan. (Hyunjin, 2004)

Me at work at Sam Kwang. That's Tiger Hong behind me. (2006)

Saipan, on the rocks. (2006)

Zhang's going away party. (I didn't drink the beer.) (2008)

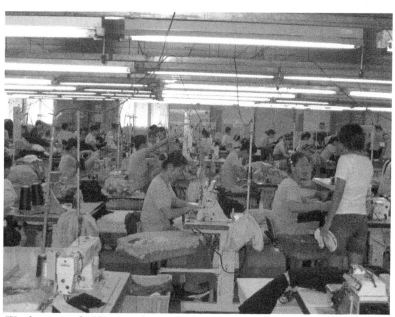

Workers inside Uno Moda, the last garment factory on Saipan (2009)

Mirage, the first factory I worked in, is now closed. (2009)

From factory girl to waitress (2009)

Me and Tiger Hong (2009)

Former factory girl! (2009)

Chapter 13: Sam Kwang ▲

March 24, 2005 to January 17, 2008

I had worked at Mirage, Marianas Fashion, Advanced-Rifu, Hyunjin, and Rifu again. On March 24, 2005, at 7:30 a.m., I arrived at Sam Kwang—the fifth factory I've worked on Saipan—with seven other girls to start my new job. They told us to sit in the office to wait for the big boss. We waited for almost two hours. Finally, the boss arrived. He told us we would have to live in the barracks. We told him we all had husbands on Saipan, so we didn't want to live in the barracks. After a few minutes, he agreed to our request. Afterwards, we all laughed about our little lie.

Then we met our director who showed us to the factory floor. She looked about 45 years old. She was fat with short hair.

The factory had five lines of about thirty girls each, spread out over two floors. Upstairs there was cutting and sewing. Downstairs, there was ironing and packing. The director put some of us upstairs and the others downstairs.

The monitor on the upstairs line was from Chong Qing. Her name was Hua. She was about 28 years old. She had long hair and big eyes. She was short and fat. She was skilled on many types of machines. The boss liked her, and would always joke with her and we would notice him touching her whenever they talked. I was assigned to her line with thirty girls all from China, Chong Qing.

Just like in other factories, the old girls made trouble for the new girls. Sometimes the new girls would get the difficult jobs, and the old girls would get the easy jobs. Since the monitor was from the same city as the old girls, you could be sure she would give them the easy jobs. If you had a disagreement with one girl from Chong Quing, the rest would take her side, and want to fight with you as well. It was like a little warring faction within the factory.

After three days, I got into a fight with an old girl named Shun. She was short and had long hair. Everybody knew her. She was dishonest and villainous. She was like Saipan's weather—one minute rain; the next minute sun; very changeable.

I cannot remember exactly what happened, but she accused me of making a mistake with some of the clothes. I wanted to answer back, but I didn't want to fuss about it. However, she continued to make trouble. She said the clothes I was sewing were no good, and threw a pile of them on my station.

I said it wasn't me. There were other girls doing the same work that I was. I had the ticket stubs for the clothes to show which ones were mine.

"I don't care who is responsible," Shun said, "I'm giving them to you to fix!"

I was very mad, and I threw the clothes back at her.

"It wasn't me!" I told her again. "Why are you giving me trouble? Because I'm new? Who do you think you are?" I asked angrily. "You'd better open your eyes and look who I am!" I threatened. "I'm not new to Saipan!"

Our voices escalated. Things were getting worse. Everybody started to stare at us. They were surprised that I was so ferocious. That's when the monitor stood up.

"Get back to work!" she said. "Both of you!"

Shun looked at me and got scared. She mumbled something under her breath—something insulting. I didn't hear it. She, too, was one who terrorized the weak and feared the strong, but after that day, she treated me better. She realized I was not one of the weak.

I have bad memories of Sam Kwang. When I think about the Sam Kwang toilet, for example, I want to vomit. There were about 400 girls working there, and there were only four toilets, and never any running water. It always smelled very foul. The bathroom door could not lock completely, so sometimes, someone would be inside, and someone else would walk right in on them.

The men's toilet was even worse. There was only one toilet for all of them. There was always someone outside the toilet yelling to someone inside to hurry up! The men's toilet was also very close to the women's toilet, allowing the men to easily see inside.

Sometimes we couldn't walk inside the bathroom because the sewer was backed up and there was urine and feces on the floor. It was nauseating.

When there was no water, we had to control ourselves until lunchtime. Then, we could go to a friend's or another co-worker's house nearby. The boss knew the conditions were like this, but didn't care. The boss' office had its own bathroom that the boss and monitors used.

By law, whenever the Department of Labor came to inspect the factory conditions, they were required to notify the boss first, so Sam Kwang always knew exactly when to clean the toilets to make a good impression. We were the ones who had to clean up the factory before the Labor Department representatives arrived.

When an inspection was announced, the boss would call the director, monitors and secretaries to a meeting. The monitors would then meet with the factory workers to teach us how to talk to the labor representatives—what to say and what not to say.

They also improved our working conditions for the occasion. For example, every machine on the factory floor was supposed to have a safety attachment to stop snapped needles from getting to our eyes or hurting our hands. We worked all the time without that protection. Most girls didn't like working with it because it blocked our vision, made the stitches harder to see, and affected our accuracy and productivity. However, the night before an inspection, they would put the attachments on our machines.

Also, they were supposed to give us masks to work. Again, we never got them until the day before Labor was coming to visit.

They would tell us to conceal exactly how many pieces of clothing we were producing, since our actual numbers were higher than what they reported to Labor.

They would hide the overtime cards, and tell us not to say how much money we earned. I believe we were working way above the time that was allowed for overtime—violating some sort of law.

We were basically told that in responding to anything that labor asked us, we were supposed to make the factory look good.

Everybody had to wear their work ID cards in plain sight. If we didn't have our IDs we wouldn't be allowed in the factory on inspection day.

The end result of all this "training" was that even though girls often complained throughout the year about conditions at the factory, when Labor representatives actually investigated the claims, they would find a factory full of safe, agreeable, happy workers. When the Labor officer arrived, they would randomly choose some girls, and call them into the office to ask questions, but their answers, and thus the labor reports would all be favorable. The girls would get nothing for their pains.

We also had inspections from potential clients and designers who wanted to hire the factory to sew their clothes. Once, a salesman from Hong Kong came to check out Sam Kwang. He had placed many orders with Sam Kwang in the past, and wanted to make sure the conditions were okay before he increased our orders. A good order could provide us work for up to six months.

The designers were scared they would lose business from bad news reports about factory conditions. So, it was important that the sales representatives for the designers check out the company first. The factory boss knew they were coming, so he told the monitors, who then told us, among other rules, not to throw anything on the floors—everything had to look clean and safe.

At about 8:00 a.m. one morning, three salesmen came from the company in Hong Kong. They checked to make sure our machines had safety attachments. They checked to make sure we had masks. They checked for broken needles.

Broken needles, by the way, were a very important issue. Every time a needle broke, we were required to take it to the monitor to exchange it for a new one. The monitors were required to keep a log of the needles. There had been many lawsuits filed by customers who were hurt by needle fragments in the clothes. Unlike some factories, Sam Kwang didn't have a metal detecting machine to check for broken needles in the clothing.

The Hong Kong salesmen checked for fire safety extinguishers and exits. They observed our efficiency. They checked if the cutting was being done safely and with properly maintained machines. They checked the packing and the ironing departments. After they were all finished, they started choosing workers to be interviewed. I remember that day they chose our line for interviews. The girl they chose was named Yong Mei. She was very short and skinny. She had her hair in a ponytail. She was very shy, didn't like to talk, and was very timid. When the monitor called her name, she immediately started shaking with fear.

When Yong Mei went to the office, she was so scared and nervous she forgot everything the monitors had told her to say and *not* to say. The salesman asked her how much money she spent to come to Saipan. She told the truth.

"I spent $3,750 US dollars," she told them.

Shocked, he asked her if that was really true.

She said, "Of course. Everybody spends a lot of money!" Some people even spend more!" she added. "Different cities had different prices," she added even further.

"Thank you. You can return to work," the salesman said.

The salesman then called the boss in, and asked if what Yong Mei had said was true. Caught in the open, the boss couldn't deny it. He had to say it was true.

Five minutes after Yong Mei went back to work, the boss called Yong Mei's monitor, and scolded her.

"I *told* you to tell them not to say how much they paid to come here!" he said angrily. "This order is now lost! Your girl made a big mistake!"

His face was red all the way to the tips of his ears. He was on a rampage. We could hear his shouting all through the factory.

Soon, the monitor came to Yong Mei's station.

"I told you to be careful when you answered the questions! I told you not to say how much money you paid to come!"

Yong Mei said, "I-I was scared. I forgot everything. I didn't know my answer would cause so much trouble." She started to cry.

We all felt angry with the monitor. What Yong Mei said was true. Why not tell the truth? I remember thinking to myself why couldn't people simply be honest. Why do they always have to lie? It was so contradictory.

Yong Mei's slip up was big, in fact. Eventually, Sam Kwang didn't get the order. As a result, many of the girls were angry with Yong Mei. They wanted the work. After that, the boss became very angry at our line, and things changed.

Six months after I started working at Sam Kwang, the boss fired the director. A month later, he hired another Chinese-Korean director. The new woman had worked before as a director at Rifu, so she came in with a little authority and experience, but she also came in with a reputation we all knew. Her name was Wu.

The Perfect Getaway

Ms. Wu had been the factory director at Rifu at a time when they had been sewing famous brand clothes, and shipping them to many countries. On the night one particular order had to be shipped, ten boxes came up missing. Ten boxes of clothes is a lot of clothes. A theft like that could not be done in one day.

Once a delivery date was set, the factory had to have all the clothing ready on that day, or else they had to pay a lot of money. The boss was very angry, but he had to act quickly. There was no time to replace the clothes.

He immediately called a meeting, and announced that whoever was responsible for the missing clothes had two hours to return them. If not, every room in the barracks would be searched. The boss believed it was one of the workers who stole the clothes. He said that if they found the clothes in someone's barracks, he would call the police and have the thief arrested.

He made the announcement at about 11:00 a.m. By noon, we all went to lunch. After lunch, no boxes appeared, so the boss told the office workers to go to all of our rooms to search.

It took them about four hours to check everybody's rooms, but still no boxes turned up. The boss was very upset. Ten boxes of clothes were very difficult for workers to steal. There was security outside, and every day the girls were watched very closely.

He soon realized that it must be either the monitor or the director who was responsible. It would be easier for them since they often worked late, each had cars, and the security guards never checked them. Only they could steal ten boxes of clothes without anyone noticing. He called the police and reported the theft. The police came to Rifu, and all stood outside. They all had guns. The boss then told a man we had never seen before to go inside the factory. When the man emerged, we discovered something really shocking. We found out there had been a hidden camera in the wall of the factory! Only the boss and that man knew of it.

When he viewed the tape, the boss was dumbfounded. He couldn't believe what he saw. He saw exactly how Ms. Wu stole the boxes. But it wasn't only her. The director, small monitor and even the packing boss were all caught on camera stealing the boxes.

The boss sent word for Ms. Wu to come to his office. When she and her accomplices arrived and saw the video, she, too, was dumbfounded. She had no idea she had been filmed. She thought she had escaped without a trace. She thought she committed the perfect crime and getaway. That little camera exposed her ugly features for all to see. She felt ashamed, and confessed everything.

The boss ordered her to return all the clothes, and then he ended her contract. However, he felt that because she was a director, he had to give her a chance to save face. If she were arrested and had her reputation soiled, it would be very hard for her to live. If people knew she was a director guilty of stealing, it would be very hard for her. Everybody would ridicule her. Saipan is very small. If something happens on the island, everybody knows. It would be hard for her to find another job, so the boss didn't press charges, and asked the police not to pursue the case.

Ms. Wu and her accomplices went to their homes—which were near to the factory, retrieved the clothes and returned them. After that day, they never returned.

Soon, however, every factory owner and just about every factory worker knew of her deeds. She was infamous.

In China, we say *a hare doesn't eat grass near its own hole*. Ms. Wu chose to do just the opposite, and paid the price. Now, she was working here. We couldn't understand why Sam Kwang's boss would hire her. Didn't he know what had happened at Rifu? Perhaps there was another reason.

*****

The Sam Kwang boss was a very short man. He was very skinny, and had small hands and small feet. He looked almost feminine. In fact, we called him "granny" because he looked like a little old woman. He wore glasses and was shifty-eyed. He wasn't a generous man. He liked to argue endlessly. He didn't have the image of a man who could be boss. He was also well over 60, but he was a playboy who liked young women.

When I came to Sam Kwang, I heard his story. He was having an affair with a young girl who worked in the office. I can't remember her name. She was pale and fat—at least 160 lbs. When they told me she was his mistress, I couldn't believe it. She was so fat. He was so old and skinny. How could they--?

Well, I guess they found a way! They spent a lot of time together. Every Sunday, and on other holidays, he would take her to Suicide Cliff or just to drive around the island for fun. They would go to McDonald's and Pizza Hut. One time they were at McDonald's eating, and someone from the factory saw them. When Fat Girl realized it, she became very embarrassed and ashamed.

Another time, the two of them went to a restaurant on the top floor of the Duty Free building, and people saw them there, too.

But all was not happiness. Sometimes during our lunch hour, we would hear them fighting in the factory office. I couldn't understand what they said because they were speaking Korean. They would fight, and shout and hit the table. They were always fighting, and it would always be a standoff. No one would win.

It was loud, and it would be hard for us to sleep. Yes, sleep. You see, there were about ten of us who did not live in the Sam Kwang barracks. We lived outside on our own. At lunchtime, everyone else went to their rooms to eat. During lunch hour, the boss told us we were supposed to leave the factory. Sometimes we would sit outside and eat. However, if the sun was very hot, there would be no place for the ten of us to sit or rest. The boss had a black heart. It didn't matter to him about the sun, or how tired we were, or where we could rest. He didn't care. In China we say, *all crows are black*, which means crows will be black wherever you find them, and evil men act the same wherever in the world they are.

Well, even though we were supposed to leave the factory, we would sometimes sleep under the tables at our stations. And, from where we were hiding, we could hear their arguments, but we couldn't say anything because we weren't supposed to be there.

*****

After several months, we didn't see Fat Girl anymore. We later heard that the boss' wife, who was living in America, wanted to come to Saipan to live with him. The boss got scared his wife would find out about his fat little secret. Now we understood why they were always fighting. He had wanted to send her back to China, and she didn't want to go. We learned the boss gave her a lot of money to go back. She was gone for just a few weeks, and then the boss' wife arrived on Saipan. But, even that didn't stop his playboy ways.

In China we say, *the old cow likes to eat young grass*. Maybe the wife was not young enough for him. Every day, "granny" would come to the factory floor to search for young girls.

Every day, during working hours, you could see him sitting with the young factory workers grinning cheerily and chatting. He also liked to touch. He touched their hair, their bottoms, and their breasts. When he touched them, many of the girls didn't protest. They would only smile and giggle—thinking they were special because the boss liked them. The rest of us, however, looked at this with disgust. We felt ashamed for them. It was disgraceful.

One morning, after we had just started work, the boss came to the station of a girl named Zhang Guan. I don't know what he said to her, but it seemed she got angry. Whatever she said back to him didn't make him happy either. He turned and walked away. The next day, he made trouble for her. He would criticize her work, tell her to hurry up, and harass her all day.

Before the fight, she had been assigned to one of the upstairs lines near his office. After the fight, he told the monitor to assign her to a downstairs line so he wouldn't have to see her every day. He made her life miserable. It goes to show that if you have power and influence, you can do anything. As we say in China, *if the king says the subject must die, it will be so.*

Once everybody knew that Ms. Wu was coming to our factory, it became the main topic of discussion. Many of us already knew how it was to work for her. Many of us knew she was vicious, sly, stern and unwavering. She was a cold-blooded animal.

Before she came to Sam Kwang, the monitor told us we only had a few days of "good times" left, because when she arrived, we would have to be very careful.

Because she had worked at many factories on Saipan, people only had to hear her name to get angry. People said she was an evil creature. *Why didn't she just go back to China?* Some people wanted her to meet in an accident. Others wanted her dead. Can you imagine how much they must have hated her?

Early one morning, just after we started working, the big monitor came upstairs and told everyone to go downstairs for a meeting. She told us Ms. Wu would be coming, and wanted everyone to meet her. Everybody already knew her quite well. We knew she simply wanted to make a show of her power and position.

When I got to the meeting, I saw her standing in front of the table. She was telling everybody, "Hurry up!" and "Be quiet!" The first thing she told us was, "Your boss invited me to come to this factory. I hope everybody will cooperate to make Sam Kwang better and more productive. Many of you know me, and my history."

She talked about work and how we should behave. "If the monitor and you have disagreements," she warned, "you cannot answer back. Whatever the monitor says, you have to listen. Even if the monitor is wrong, you must listen and obey. If someone violates this rule, they will be sent home."

She added, "If you don't finish your quota for the day, there will be no overtime. You will have only until 5:00 p.m. to finish. You cannot be absent. Even if you are sick, you have to come to the factory to ask permission to take a day off. You cannot make a phone call or tell someone else to report for you. If you violate this rule, you cannot come to work for one week. You also cannot come to work late. You must be here five minutes early to punch your time card. Anyone coming late will not be allowed into the factory."

When I heard these rules, I was very angry. I didn't want her to be our director. I had worked for her before. I knew all about her.

In China, we say *a fly cannot stop eating 'poo poo.'* I knew she would be the same as before. She was brutal, heavy-handed, callous and cruel. She would never change. She was forever a fly.

Ms. Wu's meeting lasted about half-hour. Afterwards, everybody was angry. Once we started working for her, we discovered she always had new rules and new ways of doing things.

In the mornings, she would come to check everybody's machines and the condition of the floor. If the floor was not clean, we had to stop working and sweep and clean it. She prohibited us from throwing anything on the floor, not even thread. Can you imagine? It's a garment factory! How can you not have thread or cloth falling on the floor? Every hour, we had to stop and record how many pieces we completed, and then clean the floor, and take care of the garbage. Who can do that and meet quota too?

I remember one day, early in the morning, she came upstairs

to check our machines. She came to Xiao Fang's station. Xiao Fang's machine was not clean enough, so she scolded her.

"Don't you have eyes??" Ms. Wu asked. "How can you say this is clean? You know you like to wear pretty clothes that are clean. Why can't your machine be the same way? Why can't you clean it better???"

Xiao Fang cried.

Every day Ms. Wu was somewhere in the factory shouting at somebody. She was like a loose cannon. Since she came to Sam Kwang, she pressed us constantly to meet our quotas. Every line monitor had to go to meetings to report on their lines.

She told the monitors, "If your line cannot finish your quotas, your day will end at five o'clock, with no overtime!"

She was bad luck for the workers. When we didn't make a quota, she would blame the line monitor and choose a new one the next day. We didn't know who would be our monitor from one day to the next. It was very stressful.

The monitors would get scolded every day. Sometimes they would cry. Ms. Wu didn't care whether the clothes were easy or hard to sew, she expected the same level of productivity always.

We were under constant pressure. She would scold the monitors, who in turn, would scold us. The monitors bullied the girls and became just as unreasonable as Ms. Wu. They were always shouting and fighting with the girls on the line. It was unbearable. In China we have a saying: *when fowls and dogs are together, there can be no peace.* Every day, the constant scolding and arguing was like the crowing of cocks and the barking of dogs.

Illegal Factory

It was April of 2006, and I was working at Sam Kwang. At that time, we were only working eight hours each day with two days off. There was no overtime.

Zhang, meanwhile, was working at Onwell. She, too, was working for only eight hours with two days off. Zhang and I lived close to each other, and on our off days, we had nothing to do but sit in the house all day. We both wanted to make more money, so we decided we would look for a small factory to work.

We asked a friend named Cheng to help us find factories where we could work. Cheng told us about three factories. We already knew about some of them. Some of the bosses were known to be dishonest. We knew they sometimes paid late, or not at all. Since the factory was illegal, there would be no contract. If they didn't pay you, there was nothing you could do. You couldn't go to court for judgment. Zhang and I were scared that if we worked at one of those factories, we wouldn't get paid.

At the illegal factories, there was no overtime. You got paid a flat $3.05/hour even if you worked 100 hours. Even when the minimum wage on Saipan went up to $4.05, the illegal factories still were only paying $3.05. They didn't care. They didn't have to raise their wages. There were always people who wanted the work. It was a better-than-nothing job that many people would be glad to get.

Most of the illegal factories were doing work subcontracted by the big factories. Usually, if the shipping deadline is approaching and there are not enough workers, the big factory will hire the small factory to do the work to help meet the deadline. Bosses of the factories are friends with each other.

Soon, we found out about a place in Dan Dan, in a small building near to the road. Only a few people even knew there was a factory there. All the doors and windows were covered with cardboard. No one passing by could see what was going on inside.

I had heard about it before. John's Sri Lankan friends had lived on the first floor. The factory was on the second floor. It was run by a Chinese boss from Guang Dong.

One Friday, at about 5:30 p.m., after our regular jobs, Zhang and I took a taxi to the building. When we arrived, I knocked on the door. A woman—about 30 years old, with a ponytail—opened the door. She looked very surprised.

"What do you want?" she asked.

"Do you need any people to work?" I asked.

"How do you know about this place?" she asked in reply.

"My friend told me," I replied.

After she was convinced that we were telling the truth, she let us in the doorway and talked more urgently.

She needed us to start right away. The shipping date was approaching. "We would need you to work all night until tomorrow," she said. "Can you start?"

When I heard that we might be working all night and day, I got a little worried. If I worked all night and tomorrow, maybe I would be too tired. I had been working only eight hours for so long that maybe I couldn't handle it.

Stay or go home? I could not decide

"If we work now, when do we get paid?" Zhang asked.

"After fifteen days, you can come to pick up the money," she replied. "Guaranteed. It's one-hundred percent sure you'll get your money."

"Okay, we'll stay," Zhang answered for the two of us.

She then took us inside the factory. There were three lines of machines, and about twenty people. They were working very hard. She brought me to a machine, and told me to start working.

It was a different machine than I was used to—one used to sew hems. It had been a long time since I had used it. I was nervous, but after about a half-hour, I got up to speed.

While I was working, I asked one of the girls beside me, "Is it easy to get your pay here? How long have you worked here?""Long time," she replied.

She also told me the boss was very fair and loyal.

"If you work one hour, he'll pay you one hour," she added.

"Which factory are you from?" I asked.

"Everyone here is from L&T," she replied. "He only wants girls from one factory to keep everything secret. He's scared of getting in trouble. We all heard about it through word of mouth. Did the monitor tell you not to tell anyone?"

"Yes, we had to promise her before she would let us inside," I replied. "She also told us there's not always work to do."

"If there's work, there's a lot all at one time," she said. "It's never regular."

"No problem," I replied. "I already have work at Sam Kwang, but I just wanted more income."

Inside the factory was not so bad, really. There was music playing, and we could talk to each other. Not like the big factories.

That first day, Zhang and I worked for nineteen hours from Friday at 6:00 p.m. until Saturday at 1:00 p.m. There was no break.

When we finished, our backs were in pain. Our eyes were almost closed with sleepiness. If there had been a bed right there, I would have just fallen over and slept.

After nineteen hours of hard labor, we were full of complaints. When we left that afternoon, we vowed we wouldn't do it again! That money wasn't easy, we agreed. So what if we were bored? No problem. We could deal with staying in the house. We'd just spend less and eat less!

Twenty days later, we went back and got our money. It was about eighty dollars cash. Today that building is an office building.

Looking for Bones in an Egg

My Sam Kwang line monitor's name was Ying. She was very tiny. She had a small head, small features, and a small body—all skin and bones. She wore pigtails, and she never smiled. Every day she looked as mournful as if she was at a funeral. Nobody who saw her ever got a happy feeling. She didn't have an education. She was ignorant and selfish. She overestimated herself. She felt self-important. Nobody liked her. No one wanted to be her friend.

She worked on E line before, and the big monitor liked her. That's why she got to be our monitor on F line. However, she was no good at it. She just didn't know how to be a good monitor. She didn't know how to manage the workers or oversee the tasks. She didn't understand the job, but she would always accuse us of slacking off. She would say things without thinking about how it made others feel. When she opened her mouth, it made people angry. She didn't know the proper way to speak to workers.

Ying was always making something out of nothing. She would complain to the director and the big monitor about even the smallest thing. She was always *looking for bones in an egg*—trying to find the flaw or something that just wasn't there.

I remember one time I fought with Ying. Actually, there were many times I fought with Ying. This time I was very mad with her because she accused me of lying about my productivity.

Every line had to meet a quota. We had to tell the big monitor and the director how many pieces we finished each day. Then the boss checked the quota. If we didn't finish the quota, they would end our workday at 5:00 p.m. and deny us overtime.

They would only give us overtime if the shipping date was approaching and they were worried we wouldn't meet the deadline. Ying liked money very much, so she wanted to work overtime every day if possible. If we didn't get overtime, her face would get as long as a donkey's.

To make sure we got overtime, she started making false reports claiming we did more clothes than we actually did so she could impress the boss. If there were a lot of clothes, she would inflate our daily numbers to impress the boss and get overtime. She reasoned that we could always make up the underage the next day during the overtime, so no one would notice. By the time the shipping date arrived, we would be caught up, and everyone—especially Ying—would be happy.

But while Ying was ambitious, she was not very smart. She even inflated our numbers when the orders were small, and so the lies caught up to her quicker. For example, if we had a small job of 1,000 pieces, based on the numbers she reported, the boss would expect that we finished in two days. But when he compared Ying's report to the actual tickets handed in by the girls after two days, the numbers did not match. The boss would get angry, call her into the office and scold her. She would cry, apologize, and then she would do the very same thing—lie about our numbers—that same evening.

So, on that day we had our fight, she had come to me with a question about the number of clothes I reported on my ticket.

"Where does this number come from?" she asked me.

I stopped working.

"What did you say?" I asked angrily. "Are you saying I'm lying? Go back and count them yourself. Add them up, and you'll see it is right! Why do you close your eyes and make stories? I've been here on Saipan many years, and worked at many factories. No monitor has ever said I lie on my quota. In fact, I always say that I do *less*, never more. I'm not like other girls who cannot finish and then lie about it. Why do I have to lie?" I shouted. "If I can't finish a job, I am honest about it. I don't lie. I don't like lying," I told her. "If I do something wrong, I will accept criticism. If I am right, you have to give me my respect!"

Our fight started to get louder.

"I told you to go back and check my quota cards!!" I said louder. "Why don't you go?" I wanted to prove my innocence to the whole factory. "If you don't go, I will go the office and talk to the big monitor myself!"

The other girls were telling me not to fight with her.

"You know she has no head," they reminded me. "When she talks about things she never thinks."

But, I was very angry. My body was shaking. I was indignant. Ying started to have second thoughts about picking a fight with me, so do you know what she said?

"I'm not only talking to you," she said deviously. "There are other people here I'm talking to."

Did she think I was stupid? I thought to myself.

"You're standing in front of me," I said. "You're looking right at me! If not me, then who are you talking to!?" I asked.

She turned and walked away.

Later, everybody told me, "Good job!" for telling her off. They hoped it might wake her up and let her know what type of person we knew her to be.

Another time, we were sewing winter clothes for a big job, and we didn't have enough people to finish the job. In a situation like that, one person sometimes had to use two machines to get a piece done. Can you imagine? One person sewing on two machines?

For example, under normal conditions, you might sew the buttons on a coat using the first machine. Then you pass the coat to the next girl who sews the hem. But, if you're sewing fast, and the next girl on the line is slow, or, if there are not enough people, the clothes you're working on start piling up. The monitor might tell you to go to an unoccupied hem machine. That's what happened to me. I like to do things quickly. I don't dawdle or kill time, but that put me at a disadvantage. The clothes I was sewing were piling up, so the monitor told me to start working on the second machine.

One evening, at about 6:30 p.m., I was sewing on two machines. I finished working on the first machine, and then went to the second machine. But, when I got back to the first machine, there was now a higher pile of clothes from the girl in front of me. I had just returned to work on the first machine when Ying came to me.

"What are you doing? Are you working or not?" she asked. "Why is your pile of clothes so high?"

My head was down busily working. When I heard her voice, I looked up and asked her, "Are you telling me I'm playing? Look. It's only me sewing on two machines. When I finish one, I have to go to the other machine. I'm very busy, and you're telling me I'm playing??!! Why are you always telling such bald-faced lies?" I screamed. "When you talk, why don't you think, and take a good look first!?? You always like to provoke a fight! Why do you always like to fight so much!?"

Ying said meekly, "I only say one thing, and you fight with me?" She started crying. "I can't say anything to you people?" she asked with tears in her eyes.

"When you talk about something, you have to seek truth and facts," I replied, as she walked away.

The big monitor was sitting and sewing. When she saw our small monitor Ying crying, she stood up, and called my name.

"Wang," she said, "When the monitor speaks, you have to listen to her."

"Why do I have to listen to her?" I asked. "Why is she telling me I'm playing? I'm not playing, I'm working!"

"I didn't hear her say you were playing," Big Monitor said.

"If you didn't hear what she was saying, then why are you talking to me like that? (That day was a big fight!) Don't think that just because you are big monitor that I'm afraid of you. I don't care about you. Even if you go to the boss, I don't care!"

"If you say anything more, I'll send you home," she threatened.

"No work? No problem!" I replied loudly.

I didn't stop talking, and neither did she. We argued back and forth for about half hour until the bell rang for us to go home.

She didn't send me home. My work was too important.

Big Monitor & Bigger Monitor

Our big monitor's name was Pan. She looked to be about 40 years old. She was very short, with a boyish haircut. She was top heavy, and her legs were skinny. She looked quite queer. She walked around with her arms folded behind her, giving her a commanding image, like a warden or general.

Pan had worked at L&T Factory, and had just recently come to Sam Kwang after L&T closed. She was originally the small monitor for B line, which was downstairs. But Sam Kwang had just received a big order, so the boss moved her line upstairs, combined it with our line (E), and she became the big monitor for the combined upstairs lines. (Zulen, the original big monitor for all the lines, then became known as "Bigger" Monitor! She got promoted!)

In China, we say *men cannot be judged by their looks*. This was so true for women too, and for Pan. She was not pretty. However, I heard she had three boyfriends. Boyfriends #1 and #2 were from China, and had gone back home after L&T closed.

Boyfriend #3 was from Hong Kong, and had gone back home as well. He was a young boy—younger than her by about fifteen years. He was fat and short. When they stood together they looked like mother and son. It was strange.

After she started working at Sam Kwang, we heard rumors that boyfriend #3 called from Hong Kong to tell her he missed her, and that he wanted to come back to Saipan to be with her.

One day, she was absent from work. We found out she went to the airport to meet him. The next day we saw her with a big jade necklace. She looked very happy. She showed off the necklace to everybody telling us that her boyfriend bought it for her from Hong Kong. She was quite proud of herself.

When people talked about her, it was always with a bit of disgust. Everybody thought that the age difference between them was inappropriate. We all felt he really wanted a mother, and was looking for someone to take care of him. The boyfriend didn't have a job. He stayed at home and cooked and cleaned. In the evenings, he would come to the factory on his bicycle to pick up Big Monitor to take her home. They were always hand in hand. She told us that every month they spent her entire salary.

We would tease her and ask, "How is it with a young guy?" She would blush embarrassed, but never answer us.

Since Big Monitor Pan started working upstairs, she would often make a big show of her power. Her voice was always very loud. When she opened her mouth to talk about anything, it was like a machine gun going off. It always sounded like she was fighting. She didn't care what image, or what message it sent. She was like a village woman with no etiquette and bad demeanor.

Four days after we started sewing winter clothes for a big job, Big Monitor Pan got into a fight with one of the girls from Ling Buo. This girl was about 38 years old. Her husband also worked at Sam Kwang. She had short hair and big, ferocious eyes. She was not a friendly person, and she had a bad habit of lying.

Ling Buo Girl was the first person on the line. So when, the patterns were first cut, she was the first to get the pieces. Once she completed her task, she passed them down the line for someone else to do their task. However, she always completed the same amount of clothes every hour: sixty pieces. Never more. Never less. The boss, however, wanted us to complete one hundred pieces every hour, so Ling Buo Girl was holding back production. As the first person in line, if she didn't complete more pieces, none of us could complete any more either. She was setting the pace.

A few days after the job started, frustrated with the pace, Small Monitor came to Ling Buo Girl ready for a confrontation.

"It's been four days," Small Monitor said to her. "You never sew any more than this. Why?"

"I can only do sixty pieces," she said. "I cannot do more."

She started arguing with Small Monitor, while Big Monitor was in the back watching. Finally, Big Monitor Pan joined the fight.

"I've been watching you for four days," Big Monitor said. "You are always talking with other girls. You're not concentrating on the work."

"If you think you can do more, then you come and do it," Ling Buo girl challenged her.

"Stand up, then!" Big Monitor Pan shouted, as she walked over. Pan started sewing while Ling Buo Girl stood there. All the time, all three of them continued arguing. They yelled. They cursed. They threw things. Everybody stopped working to enjoy the match. We couldn't tell who was winning because they were all shouting at the top of their lungs. I was two stations back on the line enjoying it along with everybody else.

After a few minutes, Big Boss came and asked what was happening. Big Boss, who was Korean, didn't understand Chinese, so he couldn't understand what the fight was about. He called his translator, and asked her to explain. When he understood what was happening, he told Ling Buo Girl to punch out and go home.

"And don't come to work again!" he added angrily.

Ling Buo Girl quickly gathered her things and stormed out. She slammed the door very loudly, making Big Boss even angrier.

Then, something very unusual happened. Bigger Monitor, who was overseeing the combined lines, followed Ling Buo Girl outside. We could see her close the door and start talking to her.

Everybody was surprised by this. Why was she following her outside? It was unlike her. It was not her usual personality. Bigger Monitor was the type of person who could be depended on to throw oil on a fire…..and watch it burn.

So, why would she be trying to persuade Ling Buo Girl to stay? Do you know what secret they had between them? It turned out that Ling Buo Girl and another girl had each given $500 to Bigger Monitor to work at Sam Kwang. Bigger Monitor was scared that Ling Buo Girl would go to the labor department and complain, and get Bigger Monitor into trouble.

Once outside, Bigger Monitor told her, "Go home now since the boss is very angry. But wait until tomorrow. I have an idea. I have a new plan to get you back." She was a schemer.

In a few days, Bigger Monitor told the boss that there were not enough people to finish the big order we had, and that he needed to hire new workers. She then reminded him about Ling Buo Girl, whom he fired. The boss was also scared that Ling Buo Girl would go to Labor and complain, since he knew it was illegal for him to terminate a worker's contract the way he did. If she had done something criminal, like stealing clothes, that would have been different. He would be able to fire her like that, but the way he ended her contract was not right. So, after he thought about it (with Bigger Monitor's help), he decided to *push the boat with the current*. He was too proud to admit he was wrong, and ask Ling Buo Girl to come back to work. But since he didn't have enough workers, he could do it and save face. So, going with the current, he told Bigger Monitor to re-hire Ling Buo Girl.

When she came back to work, Ling Buo Girl was assigned to work on the downstairs lines where the workers hadn't seen the fight and—or so the boss thought—didn't know he had fired her.

Now, Ling Buo Girl was not the only person whose money Bigger Monitor took. Both the Director and Bigger Monitor had been secretly working on a moneymaking scheme.

They knew that Sam Kwang's workers' contracts were expiring, and it was very difficult to find a job on Saipan. Three months before a worker's contract expired they would ask that worker how they were introduced to Sam Kwang. They wanted to know if the girl had taken the test, or if they had been introduced to Sam Kwang by someone else. If the girl had taken a test at Sam Kwang, that meant that she had no connections, and could be extorted for $500. If, however, she had been referred by someone—a monitor, office worker or the boss' friend—it meant she might have connections and power and could not be blackmailed.

At the same time, other factories were closing, which meant many girls were coming to Sam Kwang looking for work. They knew those girls wouldn't want to stay in the barracks either.

So, they began telling people that if they wanted to renew their contracts, or get hired by Sam Kwang, they would have to live in the barracks. If not, they wouldn't be renewed or hired. They knew Saipan's garment industry would not last forever, and wanted to make money as quickly as possible, however unscrupulously.

When Michigan factory closed, more than twenty girls came to Sam Kwang to register and take the test. They all lived outside the barracks, and would want to continue living outside. Director and Bigger Monitor saw this as their big chance.

One girl at Michigan Factory had a friend at Sam Kwang. "Michigan Girl" gave her friend $500 to give Bigger Monitor for a job, with the understanding she would live outside.

The girl at Sam Kwang who took the money was from Dalian. A few days later, "Dalian Girl" told her friend, "Michigan Girl," that she had made the necessary arrangements, and that she could come to work.

Three weeks later, Michigan Girl got her first check and realized the barracks and cafeteria fees were being deducted. She was confused and angry, and asked Dalian Girl what happened.

"Did you talk to Bigger Monitor or not?" Michigan Girl asked her. "Why was the money taken from my check?"

"I don't know," Dalian Girl said. "I gave her the money you gave me."

Michigan Girl decided to take matters into her own hands and confronted Bigger Monitor directly.

"What money?" Bigger Monitor replied when questioned. "I didn't get any money from you."

"You're lying," Michigan Girl said angrily. She went back to Dalian Girl and told her, "Let's go see Bigger Monitor together."

When the two of them confronted Bigger Monitor, Dalian Girl said to her, "I gave you $500," giving her the exact time and location the payoff had occurred. Bigger Monitor still maintained that she had not received any money. The three of them started fighting and shouting—each one saying she was right.

The final result was nothing. But after the fight, Bigger Monitor told Michigan Girl not to come to work. She fired her!

Michigan Girl was very angry. She had spent $500 to get a job. Now she had lost her $500, lost her job, and made only about $200 in pay. *The hen had flown away and the eggs had been broken.*

But Michigan Girl was too angry to let it go. The next day, she went to the Department of Labor to complain about Bigger Monitor's scheme. After a few days, a representative of Labor filed a notice for Bigger Monitor to appear at the Department of Labor.

When Big Boss got the notice, he felt betrayed. He had trusted Bigger Monitor. He didn't believe she could have done what she did. He talked to Bigger Monitor, but she denied taking any money for jobs. She said the workers were accusing her falsely simply because she had disagreements with them. Even so, the incident affected their relationship, and for a long time Bigger Monitor and Big Boss didn't speak to each other.

When Bigger Monitor appeared at the labor office, the representatives questioned her for almost three hours. She denied everything. She told them she never received a single cent from anybody. Labor couldn't do anything since they had no real proof.

Eventually, they released her with only a warning. If there were any future complaints like this, they told her, things wouldn't go as smoothly as they did that day.

When she came back from Labor, Bigger Monitor looked as angry as a wild horse. She immediately found Dalian Girl and changed her job. Before, she was giving clothes to the packing department and counting the ironing department's output—an easy non-ticket job. Bigger Monitor put her to work on the line. It was her way of disciplining Dalian Girl, and reminding us of her power.

The next day, Bigger Monitor called all the line monitors and workers downstairs for a meeting.

"I don't know why you people did this to me," she told everybody. "I'm kind to all of you. I never took anyone's money."

It was so unbelievable, it was almost believable. She looked as if she was about to cry. It actually looked like she was sincere, but everyone knew she *did,* in fact, take many people's money. I knew personally more than ten people who gave her money. Others gave jewelry. Did she really believe she had a pure heart? Did she really believe she could convince us of something we knew to be a lie? *Fire cannot be wrapped up in paper.* Did she think her fire wouldn't burn through the paper for all to see? There was no way to conceal what she did, at least from us. We knew. We all knew.

The meeting lasted about half-hour. She was mad at everybody. She told everybody that if it happened again, she would demand that they show proof before accusing her.

About two weeks later, Bigger Monitor didn't show up for work for two straight days. Everybody was surprised. "Why isn't she at work?" we wondered. She would usually come upstairs at about 8:10 a.m. or 8:15 a.m. every day to check on us. We were all asking around the factory what had happened to Bigger Monitor?

And then, we found out. There was a girl who lived near Bigger Monitor's house who knew what had happened, and she told us. It seemed a thief had broken into Bigger Monitor's house and stolen everything of value she had—earrings, chains, rings, bracelets, cash, everything!

We joked that the thief knew her house would be so full of stuff that she would need "help" in caring for it! Bigger Monitor, however, did not think it was funny. She stayed in her house crying for two full days. She didn't eat.

Although we could only guess at the exact amount, we had a good idea that she lost a lot of valuable property. She had been taking people's money and gifts for a long time.

Some people felt sorry for her. Some people felt that it was good that she lost it all. Some people felt it was God's retribution.

Ill-gotten wealth is easy to come, and easy to go. In China, we say *evil will be recompensed with evil*. There is justice in life.

When Bigger Monitor eventually returned to work, her eyes were huge from crying, but she tried to act as if nothing had happened. She didn't want us to know she lost so much money. I have to admit, though, that I felt a bit of satisfaction. Bigger Monitor didn't have a good heart.

*****

A few months later, it seemed it was my turn to help her regain her recently lost wealth. There were seven or eight of us who had signed our contracts with Sam Kwang on the same day. When our contracts were almost expired, Bigger Monitor came and told us that if we wanted to renew our contracts that we would have to live in the barracks.

"If you don't want to live in the barracks, you can start looking for a new employer," she threatened.

One afternoon a few days later, she called me to her office. She and another office worker asked me if I want to renew or not. I told her I did, but I asked her if I could live outside the barracks.

"Everybody has to follow the same rules. There will be no exceptions," she told me. "I will give you one day to think about it."

"Okay," I replied, and I went back to work.

She didn't give me a day to "think." If you didn't want to live in the barracks, she gave you a day to find the money to give her. If she didn't hear from you, you would be assigned to the factory barracks and have the fees deducted from your paycheck.

That evening, after we finished work, I heard the girls on the downstairs lines talking about renewing their contracts. All of us girls who had come at the same time talked amongst each other.

We discovered she had told some girls but not others. Two other girls and I who both worked on the upstairs line, got angry when we heard this. We had all come on the same day. Why were some of us getting special favors? Why did we have to live in the barracks? She had told us there would be no exceptions.

We learned that the girls who had husbands on Saipan were not asked to live in the barracks. Some people who wanted to live outside would get a marriage certificate from China to prove that they were husband and wife. Da Mei, Ying and I had no idea what to do. We discussed it among ourselves, and decided we would tell her we would move to the barracks, but then, once the contract was signed, we would write a letter to Labor stating we didn't want to live in the barracks. We felt that this plan would work.

Why do I have to give my money to her? I asked myself. *I work very hard for it. This money doesn't come easy.*

The next day, when Ying was at work, Bigger Monitor asked her again what she wanted to do.

Ying asked again if she could live outside the barracks. That made Bigger Monitor angry.

"I already gave you time to think about it!" she shouted. "But today you come with the same story. I gave you your chance. Who do you think you are!? If you don't work here, do you think Sam Kwang needs you so much that we will close?"

Ying was speechless from being scolded. Her head was down. But Bigger Monitor kept on berating her. After ten minutes, she got tired of scolding Ying, and started walking towards me. When I saw her scolding Ying, I knew if I asked the same question, I would be asking for trouble, and I would be her next target. So, I decided simply to tell her I would renew and stay in the barracks. She wrote down my name.

She then went to Da Mei's station. Da Mei told her she would live in the barracks, too.

We didn't like having to agree to this, but we couldn't do anything. It was difficult to find a job. It was best to take one step first, and then look around before taking another.

Ying, however, by arguing with Bigger Monitor, had sealed her fate. Bigger monitor didn't write her name on her list for renewal of her contract.

Over lunch, we asked Ying, "Why didn't you just say yes?"

"I just wanted to ask one more time," she replied. She started thinking aloud of the consequences, and added, "Things are getting worse on Saipan. Now it's going to be hard to find a job."

I gave her an idea. I told her to go to the office ten minutes before closing to look for Bigger Monitor, and apologize. She said she was scared.

"Don't be scared," I said. "It's just for this one time."

As it got closer to closing time, I saw Ying looking nervous with worry. At about 6:40 p.m., I went to her station to give her courage to go to the office.

"My body is shaking," she said breathlessly.

"It's just for today, and it's just for one time," I said again, supportively. "If not, you'll have to go back to China."

She got up and walked towards the office to ask Bigger Monitor to reconsider, and put her name on the renewal list. I didn't see her for the rest of the day. I left that day not knowing what had happened. Ying and I were friends as well as co-workers. I really hoped she would be able to get renewed.

The next morning, I asked Ying what happened. She told me Bigger Monitor scolded her again for half hour in the office.

"What are you doing here?" Bigger Monitor had asked.

"I decided I want to renew," Ying told her, "and move inside the barracks."

But Bigger Monitor stood on her dignity.

"Now you've decided, eh? Well, it's too late," she said. "The office already submitted the contracts to Labor. I gave you enough time, and you didn't use it. It's not me who did this. You did this to yourself. It's obvious you don't really want to work here."

Ying said she was very angry, but she swallowed the insult.

Bigger Monitor then told her, "If you want to renew, you have to go directly to the big boss. If he says yes, then you can."

So, that morning, as we talked, Ying told me she still didn't know if she would be able to renew.

"If I knew she was just going to scold me again," Ying told me, "I wouldn't have gone. I wouldn't give her the satisfaction."

The truth was, Bigger Monitor had not submitted the names and contracts to Labor. She was just making things difficult for Ying. Ying, however, didn't go to the big boss. She was too scared.

Two days later, Bigger Monitor told all the people who were renewing to go to the hospital for their checkup. One by one, she told the each of the girls to go to the medical office. Finally, when everyone else had been told, Bigger Monitor walked over to Ying's station and told her to go to medical. She had been renewed!

I saw Ying smile widely. I was so happy for her.

About a week later, an office worker gave us our barracks room numbers and our move-in dates.

Even though we were happy to be renewed, the conditions of our renewal were unfair. It didn't matter if you actually lived or ate there, if you were assigned to the barracks, they would take the money for food and board from your paycheck every week.

We had decided that if the office forced us to move inside the barracks, we weren't going to eat the food. Da Mei agreed. But, when the office gave her her room assignment, she was the first to start eating the food! But she didn't move in.

Ying, however, never set foot inside the cafeteria to eat, even though a $100 meal fee was deducted from her bi-weekly paycheck. Many people thought she was a fool.

"You are living outside," they told her. "You have to buy your own food, while Sam Kwang is cutting your money for food, too. You're spending a lot."

For almost three months, Ying never went to "dinner hell." She then wrote a letter to the head office asking them not to deduct the money from her paycheck. They ignored it. They insisted that she had requested to live in the barracks.

"If you don't eat or live there, that's your problem, not ours," they told her. "You can talk to the big boss."

Ying got snubbed every time. She got very angry. Soon, she started going to dinner hell to take the food.

Getting Sick at Sam Kwang

Just like at Mirage, Sam Kwang's big boss didn't care about the workers. If a worker got sick, he never did anything to help. However, if a small monitor, big monitor, director, or one of the office workers got sick, he would quickly send them to the hospital.

If we workers got sick, we had to write a letter to the director and have it signed and approved. If she didn't approve it, we had to go to the hospital on our own and spend our own money. Sometimes, people would get a fever and want to go to the doctor. The office would tell them to wait. Sometimes they would wait for many days and the sickness would get worse and worse. Eventually, the sick girl would have to go on her own. The factory didn't want to spend the money. It would cut into their profits.

I remember one time, my kidney started hurting me. A Chinese doctor on Saipan had told me it was edema. My back hurt, my ankles were swollen, and I could not sit without feeling pain.

I told my small monitor that I wanted to go to the hospital and rest for one day. Small Monitor said, "I cannot give you the day off. You have to ask Big Monitor."

So I went to Big Monitor to ask to take the day off.

"You have to go to the office to ask the director," she said. "I can give you the day off, but I cannot make the decision for you to go to the hospital."

So I went to the office to see the director.

"My kidney and back are paining me," I told her. "I don't feel good, and I don't have any energy to work. I want to take the day off and go to the hospital and check out what's wrong."

She looked at me for a few moments and then asked, "When does your contract finish?" I knew why she was asking me that. It meant that if I wanted to go to the hospital and ended up costing the company money, I wouldn't be renewed. They didn't want to keep people who were costing them money. Whenever anyone asked to go to the hospital, they always used that question to threaten them.

She also said, "I can give you the day off, but as far as going to the hospital, you should think about that for a while."

I was very angry, but I was *like a dumb person tasting bitter herbs*: unable to express my true feelings. I knew Big Monitor had a black heart, and no humanity. She didn't think about other people. I turned and walked away. I didn't go to work that day. That afternoon, I went to Saipan's hospital for a checkup and spent almost $250 of my own money.

I don't know why my back was always in pain. I was getting tired easily while working overtime. I was always spending money to buy medicine for myself. I could not ask Sam Kwang to pay, because I wanted my contract renewed for another year. I wasn't alone. Many people were in the same situation paying for their own medical expenses.

Wasting Away

At Sam Kwang, we sometimes had orders for winter coats. Winter coats produce a lot of dust and fibers. After eight hours, your whole body is covered with it. It's hard to get it off your clothes and skin. It gets into your throat and lungs, and inside your nose gets filled with it. If it's just for a few days, there's no problem. However, if the order is big, you might be sewing winter clothes every day for months with no filter for the dust. It's easy to get sick.

After sewing winter clothes for a few weeks, a girl named Fang started to feel uncomfortable in her throat. She started coughing a lot. At first, she didn't pay any attention to it. She drank some herbal medicine that she brought with her from China. After three weeks, however, she got even sicker.

When she first came to Saipan, Fang was about 110 lbs. After she got sick, she started to waste away, getting thinner and thinner. She asked to go to the hospital.

"It's only a cough. Why do you want to go to the hospital?" the director asked.

Instead, the office worker simply gave her some pills, but they couldn't cure what Fang had. During the day at the factory, everybody would feel hot, but Fang would feel cold. At night, she couldn't sleep, and she was always coughing. She was getting worse, but she never asked again. She was scared because she had been working at Sam Kwang less than a year, and wanted to renew.

She called home to China to tell her family what was happening. They told her that if the factory wouldn't take care of her, that she should come home. Two days later, she told the office she wanted to go back to China.

When the office learned that Fang wanted to go back to China, they quickly bought her ticket. They were happy to send her back, as it would be cheaper to pay for a plane ticket one time than to pay for on-going medical care.

A few days after Fang got back to China, she went to the hospital. They told her she had *phthisis*.* They told her she was lucky she came back when she did. If she had waited longer, she might have died.

Back on Saipan, we learned that the sickness Fang had was contagious. When the office heard that, everybody got scared. Other girls in the barracks started coughing. Fang also ate regularly in dinner hell. This made many other girls nervous. They didn't want to use the dinner hell plates, so they started bringing their own plates.

Even the boss, who regularly ate in the cafeteria, stopped going there for his dinner. He, too, was scared of getting sick.

But even after something like this, Sam Kwang still didn't change, and the boss still didn't care about the factory girls' health.

---

*A disease characterized by the wasting away or atrophying of the body or a part of the body; also known as Tuberculosis of the lungs. The term phthisis is no longer in scientific use.

Tiger Hong

I first met my friend, Yu Wei Hong, while I was at Sam Kwang. Our line had been sewing winter coats. As I mentioned earlier, the boss decided to combine her line (B) and my line (E) in order to complete a big job.

On the day the "merger" of lines happened, I saw a lot of girls coming upstairs from the lines downstairs. I looked at them. They looked at me. I saw Hong. She was tall and a little chubby. She had pretty eyes. She looked at me and smiled. *Did she know me?* I thought to myself. I couldn't remember if I had met her before. I thought about it for a few minutes, but couldn't recall if and where I had seen her.

Big Monitor assigned her to the station behind mine. After she sat at her machine, I turned to see her.

"You know me?" I asked.

"No," she said.

"I thought you knew me," I said, "when I saw you smile."

She told me I looked very kind and honest. Hong and I chatted for a few minutes, and got to know each other better.

When I looked at her, I too, got a friendly feeling. She and I were almost the same age. I was just a few months older. When we talked about things, we were congenial.

She told me she had worked at Michigan factory. She told me that at Michigan, all the office workers—small monitor, big monitor, director and boss—treated the workers fairly. When the workers had any problems or questions, the factory would do everything possible to make them happy.

"I was comfortable," she said of working at Michigan. "No one scolded anyone. When Michigan factory closed, everybody was unhappy, and no one wanted to leave."

She sighed. Her eyes got wet and her face showed despair. It reminded me of how I felt having to leave Hyunjin.

She said Michigan and Sam Kwang couldn't be compared. It was hell here at Sam Kwang. Michigan had been paradise. She said that everybody here at Sam Kwang—from the small monitor up to the big boss—was "riding roughshod and unreasonable."

She told me there were twenty girls who also came from Michigan with her. Some were told they could live outside, while others were forced to live in the barracks. She learned that if she gave money to the big monitor and the director, she would be allowed to live outside. She told me she didn't want to pay, and instead she wrote a letter to the office saying that she wished to live outside. The office girl didn't even want to take the paper. She said the office girl even told her, "We don't care if you go to Labor to complain."

As a result, they were deducting money from Hong's paycheck every two weeks. She told me she intended to fight to get her money back, and that she was collecting evidence for her case.

Hong told me about another girl who also refused to give money to the director. One day, that girl and Big Monitor had a fight. They fought for one hour. Big Monitor got very angry, and told her not to come to work.

"You tell me don't come to work? You think I have to listen to you?" the girl said. "Well, I want you to give me back the food and barracks money you've been stealing from my paycheck!"

The next day the girl went to the Federal Ombudsman's Office* to complain about what was happening at Sam Kwang.

When Sam Kwang found out she had complained, they got scared that other girls would get the same idea. They gave the girl back her money, and told her, "Don't tell other people. This is a hard time for garment factories. We don't want to lose money."

At the time, she agreed, but after a few days, all of us at Sam Kwang learned what she had done. She had told everybody!

Hong told me that she, too, and Big Monitor had a fight. Big Monitor had scolded her when she saw her talking. Hong replied that she wasn't just idly chatting, but was talking about work.

"If her sewing is no good, I cannot tell her?" Hong asked boldly, goading Big Monitor into a fight.

"I only say one word, and you say ten," Big Monitor chided.

"So, you're the only one who can talk?" Hong retorted.

"When I talk, you have to listen to me," Big Monitor said indignantly.

"Why should I have to listen to you?" Hong continued. "If you tell me to kill myself, I have to listen to that too? At Sam Kwang, you are Big Monitor, but when you walk outside the door, you are nothing!"

---

*By definition, an ombudsman is a government appointee who investigates complaints by private persons against the government, government officials, large public and private corporations, and/or print and broadcast media. The Federal Ombudsman's Office on Saipan, is part of the Department of the Interior's Office of Insular Affairs, and provides assistance to alien workers with labor and immigration complaints.

That made Big Monitor very, very angry.

"Punch your time card and go home!" Big Monitor shouted.

"Why? What's the reason I should go home?" Hong asked.

Hong told me she refused! She was right, after all. Big Monitor didn't really have a good reason for sending her home. All the girls from four lines stopped to watch them fight.

Hong told me, "Big monitor spoke loud, I spoke louder!"

Hong recognized that Big Monitor was a *bully the weak and fear the strong* type of person. Hong stood up to her, and Big Monitor couldn't do anything!

During the fight, one of Big Monitor's friends—a girl in the quality check department—came and dragged Big Monitor away. Hong told me that after this happened, a lot of people told her, "You answer back and fight, that's good!" Many people told her she was very brave, and that they were very proud of her.

"Why should I be scared of her?" Hong asked me. "The thing is, I am right. I do right, so I can speak right. There's no reason to be scared of Big Monitor."

I like people who are honest like Hong. That's the way I am. If I am wrong, I will say so. But, if I am right, and you tell me I am wrong, it makes me want to fight. Hong also told me that since that day, Big Monitor hated her bitterly, but couldn't do anything.

She said she didn't know where her courage came from. At the time, and in the heat of the moment, she simply spoke her mind. Now, when she thought about it, however, she admitted that she felt a little scared about what she had done.

Many factory girls don't like to fight. Many are scared. Many will just go with the flow, but "Tiger" Hong was different. Perhaps it's because she was born the Year of the Tiger, like me.

The Tiger Hong Revolt

In September 2007, Hong devised a plan for everybody to get together to open a labor case to complain about Sam Kwang.

At first, everybody told her yes. They all talked about doing it, but eventually they took no action. They didn't want to take the risk. Though they were unhappy, many girls *feared wolves ahead and tigers behind.* They were scared that if they opened a case, Sam Kwang might fire them, or do something even worse, and they would be worse off with the wolves, than they were with the tigers.

Hong told me she had already gone to the Ombudsman's Office, but the Chinese woman who worked in the office, Ms. Jing, said she couldn't help her.

"Why didn't you come earlier?" Ms. Jing asked. "There isn't enough time."

What she was referring to was that rumors had been spreading that Sam Kwang was going to close in a few months. With just a few months of operation left, there wouldn't be enough time to go through the process and reach a settlement.

"If you want to open a case, you can submit the papers to the Department of Labor," Ms. Jing continued. "Or, you can find a lawyer and see if they can help you."

Hong told me she considered going to a lawyer, but when lawyers help you, they cost a lot of money. The money that the lawyer was asking was almost the same amount that Hong and the other girls were seeking from Sam Kwang. She didn't know what to do. She was in a quandary. She felt like simply giving up.

Hong knew I had a connection that might be helpful. She had asked me once why Sam Kwang wasn't cutting *my* money. I had told her I had a friend in the Ombudsman's office. My friend knew the local office manager, so he called and asked for a favor. He asked her not to cut the food and barracks money from my check. The office manager knew that they really could not legally force people to stay in the barracks, and that we had every right to complain to Labor, so she agreed.

Should I ask my friend to help Hong, too? I asked myself. I liked her, but I didn't really know her that well. I knew only her outside. When you trust someone, you have to know their heart. I knew that in this world, the less trouble the better. I wanted to help, but I was scared. What if something happened, and I got in trouble?

I told Hong that my friends, Da Mei and Ying stopped talking to me, because they thought I didn't want to help *them*. But that wasn't the reason. The truth was that I didn't have the ability. I wasn't even sure if my friend could help. I felt as if I was imposing if I asked him for too much help, or to help other people he didn't know personally. In China, we say I was *just like a clay idol fording a river hardly able to save myself, let alone anyone else*. When a clay idol crosses a river, the water alone is enough to melt the clay, so it wouldn't be strong enough to support anyone else.

But, I was softhearted. We all came from one place, and had a common goal. So, I told her I would do my best to help, but that I didn't want to be implicated if any trouble arose. I also told her that she couldn't tell anybody I had helped her.

I told her I was not 100% sure my friend could help get her money back, but that I would ask him what he could do about opening a case and getting a hearing date with Labor.

The next day, I told my friend that Hong had already gone to the Ombudsman's office, but that Ms. Jing did not want to help.

"How many girls went with Hong to the Ombudsman's Office?" he asked me.

I told him three people went with her. He told me to tell them to come see him at 9:00 a.m. the coming Monday, and to bring their passports, work permits and any proof to show that their checks were being cut and that they were not living in the barracks. When Hong told the three girls that she was going to open a case that Monday, only one of the girls agreed to go. The other two girls were scared. They didn't want to be the first. They wanted Hong to be *the first generation that opens the road upon which the next generation travels*. Hong was very angry with them.

So, Hong and one girl went to the Ombudsman's Office to see my friend. In about three hours, they returned. When they sat at their machines, the other girls ran to Hong to ask many questions.

"Did they help you? Can we get our money back? Will we get in trouble?" the girls asked.

"If you wanted to know, why didn't you come with me?" Hong asked, angrily. "Why do you come now to ask me?"

Soon, everyone in Sam Kwang knew that Tiger Hong had opened a case. And very soon after that, Big Monitor had a meeting with Hong and the other girls. She told Hong to close the case, and promised that the boss would pay them their back wages. Close the case first, they said, and then we'll pay you.

Hong was not easily fooled. She insisted that they pay the money first, and then she would close the case.

"If Sam Kwang wants to pay us our money, they would pay us now," Hong said defiantly. "Why should we have to close the case first?"

Hong didn't close the case.

During the meeting, when Big Monitor said that everyone would get their food and barracks money back, many people were very happy. They felt they had benefited without having to go to the Ombudsman's Office. They thought they would enjoy the fruits of Hong's labor. However, a week later, no money had been paid.

As more time passed, people began to get restless. Sam Kwang would be closing soon. There wouldn't be enough time. One by one, they started taking off from work to go to the Ombudsman's Office to open their own cases. One day, there would be two girls absent or late to work. The next day, another girl, and so it went.

Many of the girls who filed cases fabricated stories just to get money back. Some, who were living in the barracks, simply didn't want their checks reduced, so they claimed they were living outside, but they had no proof.

Because of how obvious some of the deception was becoming, my friend at the Ombudsman's Office got frustrated. He told some of the girls, "I hope you don't believe that this money is just sitting there waiting for you. You have to show proof."

After a few weeks, the Ombudsman's Office set a single date and required that everyone who wanted to file a case against Sam Kwang had to show up at the Department of Labor Hearing Office in San Antonio. About fifteen girls showed up.

The first hearing date was set for January 26, 2008. Two representatives from Sam Kwang's office appeared, but they lied and said that the big boss was in the United States, and was not able to be present for the hearing. So, Labor set a second date of February 8, 2008. Again, at this second hearing, Sam Kwang's boss failed to show up, but this time, one of the Chinese office workers and a Korean woman whom we didn't see often, but who was involved in approving the orders, arrived with checks in the amount of $500 for all the girls who had opened the case. However, if you computed how much we were owed, it was over $500 in many cases. Some girls were angry. Others were happy to get the $500.

I was the translator for that hearing.

Each girl was called by name. She walked up and showed her identification and proof, and was asked if she wanted to accept the $500. If she said yes, she would sign an agreement formally dropping herself from the case, and restricting her from filing a future complaint about the issue.

At first, seven of the fifteen girls took the $500. The other girls refused. However, the judge said that if they didn't take the $500, and requested a future hearing, they would have to show detailed proof. At that point, some of the girls got scared, and decided to take the $500 settlement.

The hearing lasted about four hours, then we had a break for lunch, and then came back for part two. By the end of the day, fourteen of the girls—including Da Mei and Ying—took the $500.

Not everyone was happy, but many had no actual proof that they could use in a future hearing. Da Mei had receipts from money she spent at the hospital, but decided just to make her life easier.

Only Tiger Hong held out. She wanted $800. She had done the calculations, and had receipts. She was owed $800, and that was that. Sam Kwang didn't want to pay, so, the judge set another hearing date of February 28, 2008.

Two weeks later, Sam Kwang called the Ombudsman's Office, and told them that they would pay Hong $700. My friend at the Ombudsman's office called me to relay the offer to Hong. Hong told me she had already found a lawyer to help her. I suggested that since Sam Kwang had been willing to come up in their offer, that she should come down, to compromise.

After a few minutes, Hong called me back.

"I'll listen to you," she said. "I'll take the $700. I still have to pay the lawyer now."

That afternoon, Hong picked up her check from Sam Kwang's office. When she got the check, she bought a case of Coca-cola, a huge watermelon, fish, and chicken for me for my help in her revolt. When I told her I didn't want it, she thought it was because it wasn't enough. The truth was I just didn't want her to spend the money. That evening, at my house, I cooked Hong and another girl dinner, and we celebrated her victory.

Tiger Hong's revolt was successful because she had detailed proof, and kept a diary of what had happened. She had receipts. I was so proud of her. She does things so carefully. She was also very brave—not like a lot of other girls. She deserved her money.

The End Draws Near

By the summer of 2007, things on Saipan had really started to change. Because of the new labor laws concerning the minimum wage, everybody's salary was going to be increasing. That was good news for us, but not for the garment factories. They would be making less money. Many already closed and departed, and those that remained made plans to relocate to countries like Vietnam.

At one point, Saipan had thirty-six garment factories. When news first started to spread that the minimum wage on Saipan would be raised, they started to close one by one. We heard that Sam Kwang, too, was going to close, but we didn't know when. Some people heard it was December, others said November, some said January. Everybody was guessing.

According to the law, if a factory was going to close, they were required to tell us at least two months before. Some people asked the boss directly. He told them "next year," but was not specific. That could mean January, or it could mean December.

Finally, on November 20, 2007, the boss called a meeting and told us Sam Kwang would be closing on January 20, 2008.

Once everybody heard that the factory was closing, they all got lackadaisical. Our contract stated that once the factory announced its closure, we would get our remaining 60 days of pay whether there was work to do or not. We were just coming to work to kill time. Soon, people started to get bad ideas. They *thought* about stealing the clothes. Then they *started* stealing the clothes!

And they got very good at it. Some girls could steal four or five pieces of clothing in one day. I don't know how they got past the security guards outside. I remember one shipping day, we discovered we were short by one hundred pieces, so we couldn't ship the order. The factory boss had to pay a lot of money.

From that day on, the boss made a new rule: we would be searched when we left for lunch, and again at the end of the day.

There were two checkpoints we had to pass through on our way out: first, as we left the factory floor, then again at the security post at the front gate. That was two searches two times per day.

Because most of the workers were girls, (there were only about twenty men working for Sam Kwang), the boss paid two local women to do the searches. If the local women didn't show up, sometimes the boss himself, along with the director, would do the searches at the first checkpoint. They would touch us everywhere, our breasts, legs, and bottoms, to see if we were taking any clothes. It was a full body search. I had worked at four factories on Saipan, and had never experienced someone touching my body to see if I was stealing. I was very uncomfortable with it. It made me angry.

Even with the strict precautions, however, we were still coming up short on shipping day. We all knew why. It was the local girls. Because they were normally much fatter than the Chinese girls, the local girls could get past the guards without being suspected. Their big bodies and big skirts could hide a lot of clothes.

During working hours, there were no security guards at the gate, so a lot of the local girls came and went during working hours. Because they were local girls, they could come and go more freely than the Chinese girls.

Here's how they did it. There was a huge water tank near to the entrance gate. During lunchtime, the local girls would sit behind the water tank and eat their lunch. Some of the girls would hide the stolen clothes on top of the water tank, and then return to work.

At lunchtime, the gate security guards would come closer to the factory—away from the gate, and behind the water tank—to do their searches. So the stolen clothes would already be behind them. The girls would pass through the checkpoint, and then grab the hidden clothes once they were past the guards.

There was one security guard—a small Bangladeshi man—who always caught a lot of girls stealing. His eyes looked like they could see inside you—even under your clothes—and tell if you were hiding anything. He would always stop the fat girls, thinking they were hiding stolen items under their work clothes.

One day, I wore long jeans and a long t-shirt. My shirt was bigger than usual, so as I walked towards the security gate on my way out, the guard thought I was stealing clothes.

"What do you have under your t-shirt? What's that I see on your stomach?" he asked me as he stopped me.

He wanted me to lift up my t-shirt and show him. That got me very angry. Why should I have to show him under my clothes? He didn't want to let me out to go home. I was very angry.

He lifted up my t-shirt.

"Are you crazy?" I shouted as I slapped his hand. "You cannot do that," I told him. "I can sue you!"

But he saw that I had nothing hiding under my shirt, and he let me go. Still, that made me so angry.

As the days progressed, the stealing was really getting out of control, so Big Boss, Big Monitor, Small Monitor and all the office workers called a meeting.

"If you're caught taking anything from the factory," they told us, "we'll have to call the police."

Their threat might have worked, but smart, determined people can always find a way to steal without getting caught.

One of those smart people was my friend, Yi Mei. She worked at Sam Kwang for two years, and was good friends with the Director. Yi Mei worked on one of the downstairs lines. When she would see the nice clothes, she would steal a few pieces for herself and her friends. She stole a lot.

Yi Mei had a big, tall and fat body. She wore very big clothing. She stuffed the stolen pieces under her work clothes, and would use tape to tie the clothes to her leg under her pants.

One day, as she was leaving for lunch, the same eagle-eye Bangladeshi security guard was on duty. He told her to stop and show him what she had under her clothing.

Yi Mei had three different pieces of clothing taped to her body, so she removed one item and gave the guard. They had just started making that piece that same day. He took the clothing and took her to the office, where he showed the stolen piece to the boss and to the director.

The boss told her she would not be allowed to return to work. They would buy her ticket and send her to China. They didn't call the police since Yi Mei and the director were good friends (twice she had gone on vacation and brought nice things back for the director). At least she left with two pieces taped to her body.

I know two other girls who were also very good thieves: B Line Small monitor and Big Monitor. They worked together.

B line Small Monitor was from L&T. She was shifty-eyed. Her hair was cut like a man's. Her face was full of freckles, and her mouth was ugly, but she had a special gift: she knew how to make trouble. She would stir up trouble by pitting one person against another and spreading lies about one to another. She had two faces. She would ingratiate herself to you, then spread rumors about you to someone else. I don't understand how she was able to get the small monitor's position. Most likely she lied her way into it. In any case, she used her talent for deception to steal a lot of clothes.

When B Line Monitor saw which line was making the pretty clothes, she would take some and hide them in her drawer. Since small monitors had a little more freedom to move around without supervision, she used working time to go out the back door and hide the stolen items. During a single day, she could steal three or four pieces. She once told a girl that she had two big suitcases full of stolen clothes—and had already shipped some to China!

B Line monitor had friends working in the cutting room making the samples. She told those friends to make three samples instead of the usual single sample. She told her to make an additional sample for her and one for her partner in crime, Big Monitor (the one with the boyfriend in Hong Kong).

One day, when the cutting room was making pretty pants, a girl from C Line went to the cutting room to see the samples, and when she checked the pants, B Line Small Monitor got mad.

"Why are you touching my things?" B Line Small Monitor asked angrily, aware that her stealing might be discovered.

"I'm just looking," C Line Girl said. "I cannot look?" However, C Line Girl had already seen the extra samples, knew they were unauthorized, and figured out what was going on.

By that afternoon, B Line Monitor's friends had finished sewing the illegitimate samples. But, how would they get the samples out of the factory? They had a clever plan.

B Line Monitor and Big Monitor took off the pants they had worn *into* the factory that morning, and in the evening, they simply wore the stolen clothes, and walked *out*, in plain sight of the guards.

Meanwhile, C Line Girl, who had been secretly watching them all day, got angry. At the end of the day, she went to the office and reported what B Line Monitor and Big Monitor were doing. The next day, Big Boss called them into his office. He confronted them and told them what he had heard. He scolded them both.

Eventually, Big Monitor found out it was C Line girl who had reported her. She confronted her, then started arguing and fighting with her. Soon, Bigger Monitor came to break it up.

In these factories, there wasn't usually a lot of stealing happening. However, with all the garment factories closing one by one, and the feeling that everything on Saipan was coming to an end, things were different.

The big boss always thinks it's the workers doing the stealing, but the big monitors and sample makers are usually the ones. They use the nighttime and overtime hours to do their stealing. The sample-making room was upstairs, and had windows that looked out onto the back of the factory. Someone could easily throw clothing out the window down into a pick-up truck waiting below.

And one more thing about B Line Small Monitor: she also stole identities! She had used someone else's name and permit to work at Sam Kwang, so even her name was a lie! I don't know how she did it, but she was on Saipan using a different name than her own. She was over the age that most girls were selected to work, so she had to use a different identity to come to Saipan. That system is very strict in China. How she was able to do it, I don't know.

*****

Even though I was usually assigned to E Line, I once got assigned to B Line to help with their work. One morning, at about 10:00 a.m., I was busy working, when I heard about a fight.

The B Line Monitor was fighting with a C Line worker. At that time, I didn't know what the fight was about. I only heard that the C Line worker had scolded the B Line Monitor. I heard they were even hitting each other. Later, I asked one of the girls on the B Line what happened, and she told me.

The C line worker and the B line monitor had been gossiping about another girl. Then, the C line worker changed faces and told the very girl they had been gossiping about that the B Line Monitor had been talking about her. When the B Line monitor found out, she got angry and started fighting with the C Line girl.

That's how this particular C Line girl was. To your face she would say you are good, but behind your back, would say bad things about you. She was an old tricky wolf. Everybody knew it. Nobody liked her. She worked in the packing department. She was single, and about 23 years old. She also stole a lot of clothes. In fact, she had so many stolen clothes in her drawer, that when she found out that Sam Kwang was closing, she couldn't get them out of the factory fast enough by herself, and had to give them away!

One night, after work, she taped some clothes under her shirt and attempted to walk past the security guards. The guards suspected her, and told her to hand over the clothes. She refused. She bit the security guard! He got very angry and called the police. She was arrested and stayed in jail for twenty-four hours. The next day the boss went to the police station and got her released. Later, they bought her return ticket and sent her back to China. In China we say, *"what can you expect from a dog, but a bark?"*

*****

There was another girl named Hong Shao. She also taped clothes to her stomach to get them past the guards. It was easy to tell what she was doing, but she thought it wasn't visible. We all knew the security guards were being very careful about checking the girls, but she didn't seem to care. She walked right into a trap.

Eagle-eye Bangladeshi stopped Hong Shao on her way out the gate, and ordered her to take out the clothes. She got scared, immediately took them out and handed them over. The Bangladeshi told her to go to the office to be punished, but she didn't go. She ran away, and we never saw her again.

Those last two months before Sam Kwang closed were indescribable; a lot of theft, but mostly a lot of boredom. The days stretched on like years. We didn't have much work, but the boss told us we had to show up every day. He didn't like to pay money for workers he couldn't see. He would rather have us just sit at the factory all day doing nothing. So, that's what we did.

Chapter 14: And Still There Are Tigers

▲

It was January 2008. Sam Kwang was officially closing in about twelve days. Most people wanted to stay on Saipan, so they were all looking for new employers. They asked their monitors for time off to go to take the test to qualify for other jobs.

Some people were lucky and passed the test. Some people, who worked ten years or more, didn't pass the test. There were about eight or ten girls from Sam Kwang who went to USC Factory to apply and take the test. They passed and were offered jobs. But, then, a week later, USC canceled the test requirement and withdrew the job offers for those girls.

The reason was that many Rifu girls were also applying to USC for work since Rifu had closed at the same time. The USC boss and monitor were money-hungry. They made it known that the only way you could get a job at USC was by paying $500. With all the girls looking for work, the boss and monitor could do quite well.

Da Mei and Ying both wanted to get new jobs. They went to Rifu II, but were told they weren't hiring. They had gone to USC, but didn't pass the original test. Afterwards, they went to MGM. At MGM, they learned that if you passed the test, you could work, but you would be on probation for three days. If, during those three days, your sewing output was more than their current workers, they would hire you. If it was less, they wouldn't hire you.

Da Mei and Ying both wanted to work at MGM, so they needed three days off in order to prove themselves during the probation period. So, they made up a story. They had another girl tell the big monitor that they had been in a car accident, were in the hospital, and so couldn't come to work. They then used that time to start working at MGM.

After three days, Ying passed the probation requirement, but unfortunately, Da Mei did not. She was very unhappy. Being a true friend, however, Ying thought that if *she* went to work at MGM, that Da Mei would be mad at her. So, even though Ying had passed, she decided not to take the job out of loyalty to Da Mei.

Even though the Saipan economy was bad, many of us didn't want to go back to China. We wanted to stay, but it was hard for us to get new jobs other than factory work. The first reason why was the language. Many of us did not speak English. Second was simply that we were Chinese. Locals got first choice of jobs.

To Stay...

Many girls tried a thousand and one different tricks and means to be able to stay. Some went to Garapan to learn how to give massages. Some became "forty-dollar girls," selling their bodies to men. Some paid business owners and individuals $1,000 or $2,000 to "hire" them so they could get a contract and a permit to stay. In those situations, there was no real job, and no salary, but with the work permit, they could legally stay on Saipan. They could then work illegally, or simply wait for the new immigration regulations which we all hoped would help us so-called "guest workers" get improved status, or maybe even green cards!

With no job, Ying and Da Mei were getting more desperate to stay on Saipan. They heard about a Chinese man on the island who promised he could get them work permits. First he told them it would cost $1,200. After Da Mei and Ying had each paid half of the money, he demanded more or else he wouldn't do it. They asked for their money back, but he wouldn't give it to them. So, they had to pay the extra money. In total, they each paid him $1,600 for help getting a permit. When they went back to find out what was happening, he denied ever receiving any money from them.

They felt cheated, disheartened and angry, but there was nothing they could do. They couldn't go to the police. They couldn't report him. They couldn't sue him. This happened to many girls.

...Or To Go?

At the same time, we all knew China's economy was improving, and was probably better than Saipan's, but many girls would still rather stay on Saipan. Even I felt the same way.

In China, I have a family, a child and a lot of responsibilities. Every day I work, and have to be responsible for everything. In China I felt like I was always working, and I was always the housekeeper. There was no time to enjoy life.

On Saipan it was just me. If I want to eat, I eat. If I want to sleep, I sleep. I have my freedom.

And maybe the other reason was that I've now lived here on Saipan for so long, that it has become a special place with special feelings for me. Saipan has beautiful oceans, different flowers, different trees, and natural beauty. In the mornings, I like to walk on the beach and just enjoy seeing the limitless ocean. There are different fruits I can taste. There are a lot of people from different countries. I can learn about different customs and traditions. I've met Americans, Koreans, Japanese, Bangladeshis, Filipinos, and many more. I have relationships I've become attached to.

A Difficult Choice

I have been here on Saipan since age 25. In those nine years, I have been through many changes. When I came, I was young and ignorant about the world, but now I have matured a little bit. I understand the value of life. I have gained a lot of wisdom about human nature. I have a clearer idea of what I want, and I also know what I *don't* want.

It is a very complicated and heartbreaking choice to make. In making it, I feel sorry for my son. He is now 11 years old. I know I've not been a good mother. I didn't do my motherly duties. I left him when he was two years old, and so I didn't give him much love. For that I am very unhappy, but I hope that when he grows up he will be able to understand. I did not love his father, so how could we stay together? Even if I went back to China, and we got divorced, I would never be able to have him.

You see, in China, men love their sons. It is difficult for a woman to get custody of a son after a divorce, especially if she is the one who initiates the divorce.

My son is also my husband's parents' first male grandchild. This makes it even more difficult for me to have custody. They would fight me all the way to keep him.

The truth is, his father and I have never seen eye to eye. I recall three phone calls during those nine years that remind me how far apart we were and continue to be.

Call #1

It was about a year after I had come to Saipan. I was working at Mirage, and had a friend who was coming from China to Saipan. I called my husband and asked him to buy something for me —some clothes, and some flower tea—to send with my friend.

When I asked him for help, he said he didn't have time because he had to work. When I heard him say he had no time for me, I felt very sad and angry.

"If you don't have time, okay, no problem," I said, and I hung up the phone.

That night I cried for three hours.

Call #2

There was another time, shortly after I had returned from my one visit to China, that I called and asked him to help me buy some medicine for my feet. Back in China, after I had given birth to my son, I developed ring worms in my feet. The medicine I needed was not available on Saipan.

When I was in China getting my ID and passport, things were so rushed that I hadn't had time to get the medicine myself.

He told me it was impossible to send medicine to Saipan. He told me the postal authorities would confiscate it. But, I personally knew of others—my friend's father—who had bought medicine in China and had sent it here.

"My friend here has gotten medicine before," I told him. "Can't you go to the post office and just ask? If you don't ask, you don't know for sure."

"Cannot is cannot," he said. "Why do you want to argue?"

"You say cannot. Okay, forget it," I said, and hung up.

I felt so wronged. I phoned my mother. I told her what happened, and told her, "I want a divorce. I don't want to be with him anymore."

"Don't be silly," my mother said. "What's wrong?"

"Why do I have a husband if he can't do anything simple for me? He never helps me with anything," I cried. "It's not just this time, it's *all* the time. It's so disappointing to live like this. If this is what it's like to have a husband, mama, then I don't want it."

My mother did not take me seriously, but said she would call my husband to ask what had happened. My mother called him and scolded him.

Afterwards, when we talked again, he told me he would go to the pharmacy, buy the medicine and send it to me. To this day, I've never received it.

Weeks later, he told me he sent it, but that like he said, the post office had taken it. I don't believe him. I think he lied.

Call #3

Whenever I called my house, my son knew I didn't want to talk to his father, so he would quickly rush the phone to him and put us together. This time I said, "No, no, no! I want to talk to *you*."

The previous time we spoke, my son had told me that they didn't have money in the house. My husband's father told my son to ask me to send them money. However, when I went to wire the money, I discovered I needed my husband's bank account number in China, so I called back to get it. This time my husband answered.

"Why are you calling?" he asked coldly.

"Because your father told your son to ask me for money," I said. "Your son said you didn't have money to pay the phone bill, and that I should send money. I need your bank account number."

"We have money. We don't need your money," he said.

"So why does your father keep telling your son to send money?" I asked. "If you say you have, and don't want, then I'm happy for you. Next time, don't ask me again."

There was an awkward silence.

"If we don't have anything to say...." he began.

"Nothing," I said.

We hung up.

Every time I called after that, there was always some underlying argument or tension. Every time I would call my parents, they would ask me, "Did you call your house?"

"Yes, I already did," I would lie. The truth was, I was not calling my house. It was too depressing. It was a constant reminder of my unhappiness. I don't want to always be unhappy and sad. I would call once a month, sometimes only once every two months.

Going back to China would mean returning to that life. I feel as though I am in a very difficult situation. On one hand, I want to go back to China—my homeland. That is where my mother and father are. That is where my heart shall always be. But the truth is, I do not love my husband. I got married not for love, but for a silly, childish reason, and because of society's pressures. But unlike Saipan, in China there is not the freedom to undo those decisions alone. There is always family pressure and societal pressure that makes everything more complicated.

Yes, still there are tigers.

Chapter 15: The Last Day ▲
January 7, 2008

The Last Day

The last day at Sam Kwang garment factory was Monday, January 7, 2008. We arrived at the factory at about 9:15 a.m. People were sitting on the tables. Some were standing around. Everyone was just idly chatting.

Even though this was the last day, we had actually sewn our last clothes a few days before on Friday, January 4, 2008. Now there was nothing to do. We were all just waiting for the boss to arrive.

The upstairs line where I worked—Line E—was the first line to finish back in December, so the upstairs floor of the factory was now closed. The twenty girls on my line were then assigned to work on the downstairs lines. As each line finished their last batches of clothes, the girls were moved around the factory to help with other tasks. They would send us to the packing department to help with the ironing and packing, or tell us to help the next line of girls clean their machines. Others were moved to other lines to sew. There was always work to be done.

To be as efficient as possible, everything was done on the same day we finished our last piece. As each line of girls finished, they would clean their machines—that would take about ten minutes. Then the packers would come and disassemble the machines, paint them to look like new, then pack them in boxes, and take them away to be shipped to Vietnam.

I ended up being on B Line sewing until the last day. B line was the very last line of garment workers to finish on that Friday. They then told us to take Saturday and Sunday off.

Now that it was Monday, we were back to hear the boss' official announcement. We waited almost two hours. We were all anxious because we all wanted to go home.

When the boss arrived, Big Monitor went to ask him what she should tell the factory workers to do. Would we continue to show up for work, or would we be sent home for good? After a half-hour, she returned and called a meeting.

"Big Boss has said that starting today," she began, "there's no need for you to come to work. Today will be our closing day."

When we heard that we were all happy. But many still voiced their unhappiness with Big Boss.

"It's about time," some said.

"You should have let us go a long time ago," said others.

"Mean, old man!" some sneered.

"Now you have to pay us," others said.

We still had two weeks until the sixty-day period was up, so we knew he was reluctant to let us go. Now we would get two weeks' pay without working. We all went to the office to pick up our checks.

That day, on their way out, girls stole a lot of Sam Kwang supplies. Cloth, thread, anything that could be taken was taken.

As we were about to leave, Tiger Hong asked me to wait for her as she had some final business to attend to. She had told Big Boss that she wanted to go back to China, and wanted to find out the status of her ticket. The office worker Hong spoke to didn't know anything about Hong's request, so she gave Hong a number she could call in a few days. Then, at about 11:30 a.m., Hong and I walked out of Sam Kwang factory for the last time.

I had brought my lunch that day, and had made a lot of food. So we walked to the rear of the Labor Department building, and had lunch in the parking lot. After we ate, we went home.

We were quite happy, but also a little fearful. We could rest for a while, yes. But we had to start worrying about what to do for money. All the factories were closing. What would happen next?

The Promise

Garment factory work is very hard work. Every second, of every minute, of every hour you have to work, very fast, and very carefully. I had been doing it for fifteen years both in China and on Saipan. There was good and bad, and a lot of trials and hardship.

However, Hong and I felt the same way about it. We had tasted the sour, the sweet, the bitter and the hot. So, on the day Sam Kwang announced it would be closing, we promised each other we would never work in a factory ever again. Even if we couldn't find any other jobs, never again would we choose to be factory workers.

One More Time?

That Monday, however, as we were walking away from Sam Kwang for what would be the last time, and before we actually made it to the Labor building to eat our lunch, Hong and I heard someone calling to us from behind. It was Big Monitor. She asked Hong and me if we wanted to have a job at an illegal factory.

Hong and I immediately said no, we didn't like the idea having just made our "never again" pact.

"Why not?" Big Monitor asked. "You'll just be staying in the house with nothing to do. Why not make some money?"

The boss of an illegal factory had asked her to look for workers for him. She told us that the factory was very near to Sam Kwang, which would be convenient for us.

We told her we already promised each other we would never work in a factory again.

"Why not just try it one more time," she asked again. "If you don't like it, you can always quit."

She talked to us for a long time trying to persuade us. Eventually, we agreed.

"Are you sure, now?" she asked finally. "If so, then tomorrow at 8:00 a.m., I'll wait for you outside the factory."

The next morning, at about 7:15 a.m., I rode my bicycle to Hong's house. I waited for her for about ten minutes. Hong came down from her fourth floor apartment.

Her bicycle was in a small shed next to the house. She took it out, and we discovered it had not just one flat tire, but two.

"Last night they were full of air," Hong said, confused.

We took her bicycle to the shop to fill the tires. When we put the air in, we discovered it was still flat, so we left it at the shop, and walked together to the factory.

By now we were running late. It was already almost 8:00a.m. We were upset, but there was nothing we could do.

We got a call from Big Monitor asking why we were late.

We were walking and running. In about fifteen minutes, we arrived at the illegal factory. The factory boss was outside. His face was very cold and icy.

"Why are you so late?" he asked sternly.

When I heard him speak so mean to us, I got very angry.

How dare he talk to us like that, I thought to myself. It was our first day. In fact, we hadn't even started yet. In fact, we hadn't even really decided if we wanted to work there!

Hong, however, was patient with him.

"Next time we won't be late," Hong told him. "The bicycle was flat, that's why."

"Since you're late, we don't have any available machines here," Big Monitor told us. "You'll have to go to another location."

"Where's the other factory?" we asked her.

"Koblerville," she told us. It was very far.

"If you don't work, what will you do at home? Play?" he asked sarcastically.

"Don't think too much about it. Let's just go," Big Monitor said, as she pushed us towards the car, while the boss got in the driver's seat.

The boss was about 35 years old, and had been on Saipan many years. He and his father, who were from China, Guang Dong, had opened a small factory years before. The father's girlfriend and the son's girlfriend didn't get along. The father's girlfriend had a black heart. She wanted to control everything.

Apparently, father and son had a disagreement that ended the partnership, and they went their separate ways. However, the father's factory soon went under. The girlfriend stole all his money. Now, he worked for the son.

The son was truly a playboy. He had a girlfriend, *and* a wife. The girlfriend was working for him in the factory office.

We drove for about ten minutes and arrived at a two-story building in Koblerville. There was no name or any sign outside. All the doors were locked and the windows were covered. There was no way to tell what was going on inside.

The boss was the only person with a key. As we walked in, I saw about twenty women and two men all hard at work.

The boss called the monitor inside and told her to show us what machines we would be working on. I would be working on a machine sewing hems. There were stacks of clothes on both sides of the machine waiting to be fixed.

"Do you know how to use that machine?" she asked.

"I used it at Advanced," I told her. "But, it's been a long time since I worked on one."

"Be careful," she said. "If you're not careful, you'll cut the clothes. (The truth was, later, while I was working on it, I actually damaged two dresses, but I quickly hid them and never told her.)

She assigned Hong to a station about five spots behind me.

It was an air-driven machine. After a few minutes, the air supply stopped. The boss called one of the men to fix it. While my machine was being fixed, the boss told me to work on cutting the loose threads from the pieces I had worked on. Once the machine was fixed, he told me to return to my original assignment.

After another ten minutes, the needle started giving trouble.

It was an old machine. At that moment, I felt I wanted to quit. I didn't want to quit right away, though, I decided. I waited a long time for someone to come to fix it. Again, while I waited, he told me to go to another machine to work.

This machine was at the station right in front of Hong. Once I got close to Hong, I asked her opinion.

"Do you want to stay, or not?" I whispered.

"It's very far to travel every day," Hong said. "It's very hard to get to work. The work is okay, but it's just too far."

"I don't want to work here anymore," I told her. "I think I'm going to just go home in the afternoon."

Once Hong heard my plans, she changed her mind.

"If you're not coming, then I won't come either," she said.

We had promised each other and swore we would never work in a factory ever again. We wanted to be truthful to ourselves.

Even looking at the machine made me unhappy. From the moment I walked into that illegal factory and saw the sewing machine, I felt a wave of unhappiness. My interest and motivation wasn't there anymore. I had stopped being a factory girl.

"No problem," I said encouragingly to her. "No money? No problem. We'll survive."

We decided we would leave at lunchtime. It seemed on that day that twelve o'clock took the longest time to arrive.

*****

At 12:00 noon on Tuesday, January 8th, 2008, I stitched the hem of a dress I was working on, removed it from the machine, and tossed it into the bin next to my station. There were still a lot of dresses piled up waiting. I turned off my sewing machine and got up from my station.

Hong finished her piece, and joined me as we walked to the office to talk to the boss. Big Monitor was there with him.

"We don't want to work here anymore," Hong told him. "It's too far from where we live, and we don't have a car to drive."

"Okay. It's up to you," he said. "If it's too far, no problem. If the factory near to Sam Kwang has machines available, we'll call you," he said.

"Okay," we said. We had no intention of ever returning.

We called a taxi to take us home, and waited in the road outside the factory for a long time for it to arrive. By about 1:00 p.m. we arrived at my house in Chalan Kanoa.

Hong stayed at my house all afternoon. I cooked for her, and then, that evening, she went home. That was the last day that Hong and I ever worked in a factory.

The Way I See it

In all, I have been at six factories here on Saipan—Mirage, Marianas Fashion, Advanced, Hyunjin, Rifu, and Sam Kwang. From my experience, if a person is good looking and speaks well, they have the advantage to go anywhere they like. The boss will like them. The machine men will help them. The monitors will give them the best jobs.

If you are too honest, too quiet, ugly, naive or too reserved, people will take advantage of you. From the first day at a factory, the monitor and other girls size you up and judge your personality. If you don't talk back, if you don't stand up for yourself, they'll keep putting you down. Their motto is *bully the weak and fear the strong*. If you are not among the strong, you will be bullied. I still will never understand why people want so much to pull others down.

And while I am wiser and stronger for having lived it, factory life is not a way of life I wish to continue.

I am glad it's over.

Chapter 16: The New Me ▲
2009

A Light at the End of the Tunnel

After Sam Kwang closed, my life on Saipan came to a stop. I didn't have a job, so I stayed at home every day. It was very boring. I was taking English language classes at college on Sundays, but other than that, things were very slow.

I used the time to think and hope. I wanted a different life—a life of substance—but I wasn't sure if that was even possible.

Then, one morning, as I took my dog, Fifi, running on the beach as I had done for many months, I met an American man who was also walking on the beach. He and another man were on the beach with two dogs. One of his dogs was the same breed as Fifi, and the two started playing together.

"Good morning," he said to me in English.

"Good morning," I replied.

"Where do you work?" he asked me.

"I don't have job," I replied. "I stay in the house."

"How do you live?" he asked.

"I have some money I saved from before," I replied.

"Do you want a job?" he asked.

"Of course, I do!" I replied.

"He told me he might be able to help me, but he wasn't yet sure, so I told him thank you, and we said goodbye.

From the beginning, I didn't know exactly what kind of job he was offering.

A few weeks later, while on the beach, we met again.

"Do you have a job, yet?" he asked again

"No, I still cannot find one," I replied.

He said he was leaving for Guam, so we said goodbye.

A few weeks later, I met him yet again early in the morning while running with Fifi. Again, he asked me about my job situation, and asked me to walk with him.

He asked me about myself, and what I had been doing on Saipan. He told me he had a restaurant. I didn't quite understand the name of the restaurant. He apologized, and said that unfortunately, there were already enough people working there, so he couldn't hire anyone new at that time.

"No problem," I said. "You've helped me just by offering."

Again, we said goodbye.

A few weeks later I met him again at about the same time.

"Jobs are very hard to find now," I told him.

He told me he had been to China and had just returned. He said he was sympathetic that I had still been without a job. He told me where his restaurant was, and that the next day at 2:15 p.m., I was to go there for an interview if I was interested.

When I heard this, I was very happy! I told him thank you.

"Don't forget... tomorrow afternoon," he reminded me as we said goodbye. "And good luck!"

That night, I tossed and turned in bed. I had butterflies in my stomach. I was nervous and worried. What if I couldn't pass the interview? Is my English good enough? I was happy, but also very scared. The night passed too long.

The next day, I got to the restaurant at 2:10 p.m. I went inside and saw the American man talking to another person. When he saw me, he got up and spoke to me.

"You're already late," he told me.

I was not late, I thought. I saw that the clocks in the restaurant were set a few minutes ahead.

"Sorry," I said.

One of the restaurant workers was asked to take me to an office in Garapan for my interview. First, however, he had to run an errand, so I sat in the restaurant and waited for about half hour.

Afterwards, the worker returned and took me to the Garapan office where I met the manager. He told me what the American man had told him about me, and asked me many questions.

He told me that he could not decide on the outcome of the interview. He would have to call the boss, and then call me to let me know the decision. After my interview, the worker took me home.

I thought about that interview for the rest of the day. Would they hire me? Did I speak English well enough?

I didn't hear from them the next day, or the day after that.

Three days later, at about 9:30 a.m., I got a phone call. They told me that the boss would hire me. When I heard this, I was so happy, I started jumping.

Over the next few days, I bought the clothes I would need for work, and I moved in to the barracks. I was about to start a new life—this time not as a factory girl, but as a waitress at a restaurant!

I really believe the restaurant still did have enough people working there. I think that kind, American man, Robert Jones of Triple J—the light at the end of my dark tunnel—just took pity on me and wanted to help me survive. For that I am grateful.

Me, the Waitress

I like my new job. I meet new people from different countries every day. Sometimes it's really enjoyable. One problem, however, is that I feel a lot of pressure working there. My coworkers are mostly all Filipino. I'm the only Chinese person working there. It's very different from working in the factory.

Sometimes I really don't understand why people can't be genuinely and sincerely friendly. Most of the girls are narrow-minded, back-stabbers, always acting out of self-interest. I feel so tired for them. It must be a lot of hard work to always be stabbing people in the back.

One minute, three friends are talking nicely with each other, but as soon as one walks away, the other two start talking about the one who just left in petty and mean ways. Of course, there are petty people in China, too. But it seems my co-workers here just like to make problems for each other. They like to talk about each other, and anyone else for that matter.

There seems to be a lot of jealousy. If someone appears to be getting ahead, everyone else gets jealous, starts talking bad about them, and gives them mean looks.

Sometimes, the slightest little thing will be turned into a big issue to be talked about over and over. Once, shortly after I started working there, my pay stub—which, along with others is delivered to the restaurant for the manager to distribute—showed my hourly salary as $4.55/hour, instead of the $4.05 it was. Apparently, someone had made a mistake in typing the information. The manager quickly told the other girls, and for a whole week, everyone—including the manager—treated me mean, started telling lies to the boss about the quality of my work, and made me cry.

It seems as if the goal here is to get the other person in trouble. They seem not to like each other at all. It's very hard for me to understand. Maybe that's just the way it is in their home. Chinese style is not like this at all. In the factory, we only did our jobs. We didn't talk about each other like that, or try to get people fired.

It seems nothing I do can make them treat me nicely and honestly. We're all from different countries, living and working together here on Saipan for just a few years. Why can't we all be happy and friendly? If everybody could just give a little love to each other, the world could be so much better.

*****

On the bright side, restaurant work is easy compared to work in a factory. In a factory, you work every second of every minute of every hour. You work continuously, sitting in the same place all the time. As a waitress, we can walk around. In the morning, we have to clean the floor and the tables to prepare for the day. Once everything is cleaned, our time is free, until the customers come in, then we take the orders. It's much easier work, plus we get tips as well as salaries.

Being a waitress means dealing with the customers to make them happy. Most customers are friendly and not fussy, but some customers can be quite mean and demanding.

Even though the work is easier, there are things about factory work that are a little better. When I was working in the factory, we always had overtime. If I worked every day in the factory, and worked overtime, I would make more than I make now. At the same time, one great thing about restaurant work is the tips. If I was able to work the same hours as I had been able to work at the factory, the tips would make the restaurant job better by far.

However, it's really not fair to compare since things are different now on Saipan. The economy is worse. And the truth is, overall, just having a job makes me grateful.

Chapter 17: Will the Last Factory Girl to Leave Saipan Please Turn Off The Lights? ▲

Forever Good-Byes

It's now February 2009, exactly nine years since I first came to Saipan. I've met many people during those nine years here. For all those who befriended me, I hope I will get a chance to see them again. Of course, those who were mean to me, I really don't want to see *them* again, but I hope they have a better life and a better future. For those who died while they were here, I hope they find peace. For those who lost loved ones in China while they were here working to make a better life, I hope they find solace.

Some people made a lot of money to go back to China. Others did not do so well, and many have returned to lives they do not like. Many live in the country, where it is very hard to make money. Many have returned to marriages and family situations that they wanted to leave behind. I feel sorry for them.

Sometimes it makes me sad. Saipan is probably the only chance we could have to see and be with each other. China is so big, that even if we were all back in China together, we live so far apart, that I don't think we would have the opportunity to ever see each other again. This was just a small moment in our lives that is over.

All the seventeen girls who were with me on my original flight to Saipan in 2000, returned to China when Mirage closed. I don't have any information about any of them. We really didn't know each other as well as we could have. Ying and I are the only ones from Mirage who are still here on Saipan. Ying is also having a hard time finding a new job. She stays in the house with nothing to do. I heard that she too may be going back to China since Labor gave her only thirty days to find a new employer. If she cannot, she will have to leave. Like many girls, she doesn't want to go back. Her husband in China was always drunk, and hit her. She's scared to return to that life. She's not sure what she will do.

One by one, many of the friends I've made on Saipan have returned to China. On December 19, 2007, it was my best friend, Zhang. It was a valuable friendship that I was sad to lose.

She wanted to leave Saipan, as she had gotten tired of living here. Everything had become too unhappy for her, and if she stayed, with no job, she would eventually lose everything. At the same time, she was unhappy about going back. Life there was sad and lonely, and she was not hopeful about how things would turn out.

Da Mei left Saipan in June 2008. I've since lost her number. Ying told me that she's working in a factory somewhere in China.

Tiger Hong wanted to go back to China, but her boyfriend on Saipan objected. She wants to find a job here on Saipan, but it is very hard. We keep in touch by phone and get together sometimes.

I heard that Old Turtle (Advanced Textiles) is back in China. She had sent all the money she earned on Saipan to her husband in China. He used the money to buy a new house, and then divorced her. He's living with a new woman. She now has nothing. When I heard this, I couldn't believe it.

Hua, Hyunjin's nice big monitor, went back to China, took a few months to relax, and then went to another country where she is a monitor at a factory.

I saw Sam Kwang's small monitor—my line monitor—at Payless Market just a few weeks ago. She told me she was going back to China for good.

I saw Martinez, the swindler, just last week. Every time I see him, I get very angry.

As I think about the many people I've met during my years here on Saipan, I think of one, in particular, that makes me very sad.

"There once was a kind machine man..."

His name was Cheng. I had been at Mirage less than a year when he came to work there. He was from China, Guang Zhou. He was tall and skinny, and black. He was very kind and easy to talk to. He wasn't like the other machine men I had met over the years. When the girls would call him, he would come quickly, and with a smile. Sometimes, when there was nothing to do, he would sit and chat with us as we worked.

One day, he sat next to my station. He told me he had been on Saipan for three years. He had a son in China, but was divorced.

I asked him who took care of his son, and he told me that his mother did. He sent money every month to help her buy clothes and food. He also told me that he had lost all his money.

"Where's your money?" I asked him.

"It's helping other people," he said.

I found out that meant he lost it playing poker.

"Well, don't play again," I told him. "Poker is like a pit. Once you fall inside, you can't get out. No one makes money at it."

"I know," he said. "But I can't stop."

Three months after he came to Mirage, things got quite slow. There was no overtime, and we had two days off each week. Everybody was bored.

I don't remember whether he really wanted to, or if it was a friend who convinced him to go, but Cheng used one of his days off to go fishing. So, one Sunday morning, he and a friend went to Bird Island with their poles and bait. That day, the weather was very bad, and the wind was very strong, but they went anyway.

While they were fishing, a huge wave came up and swept Cheng off the rocks. His friend saw him fall in the water, and disappear. He never came back up. Perhaps he hit his head on a rock, or was just swept away by the current. The waves were too rough, and his friend couldn't help him.

Cheng, the only kind machine man I ever knew, couldn't save himself. He was simply, and very sadly washed away at sea. They never found his body.

The next day, when we heard what happened, we couldn't believe it. It was so sad. Cheng left a young son and an elderly mother with no one to care for them. We all hoped that in the next world, Cheng was having a better life.

Chapter 18: From Saipan, with Love ▲

A Nine-Year Journey Made Special

In the nine years I've been on Saipan, I've experienced many emotions. I've been happy, sad, afraid, and angry. I've tasted the sweet and the bitter. I've lost a lot. I lost my money and my youth—I've been here since age 25.

But I've also gained a lot. Living in a foreign country, I've experienced many new customs and traditions, and met many unique people. I've gained friendships, and I've gained confidence. Supporting myself and my family for these nine years has made me more mature and helped me to grow and improve myself. I've seen a world beyond China that is a spectacular and splendid place.

I know now that when you seek happiness, the road can be long and the process can be difficult, but you have to persevere. You have to be relentless. As my brother's friend Guang told me two days after I first arrived, *you have to have patience.* I, too, now believe one day if you have the patience you can have a better life.

My life is, in fact, better than before. If I judge it based on how much money I saved, I couldn't say it is better. I've lent most of it to other people and lost it all because of my trusting nature.

If I judge it based on my current job as a waitress, things could be better there too. It's good to be earning a living, and I am grateful to my employer, but sometimes the people I work with can be difficult to understand and get along with.

However, as I look back, I can say that all of the sadness, and the pain and the loss, and the stress was worth it.

Why?

I met someone nice.

A Very Special Thank You

I want to wholeheartedly thank a very special man.

He gave me the idea to write this book, and honestly, without his help, I don't think I could have done it. There were times I wanted to give up, but he gave me the strength and courage to continue. Together, we went back to relive the joyous and painful times of my life. Because of him, I now have this opportunity to let people know what life as a factory worker is really like, how difficult life can be in a foreign country, and to share my experiences and feelings with the world. I shall never forget this experience and all that he has done to make it happen.

And to that special man:
When I am sad and during times of pain and unhappiness, you give me advice and encouragement. When I have difficulties, you teach me how to cope and overcome adversity. You teach me how to stick to my principles. You give me confidence. You taught me how to set goals. You are the light on my path that gives me hope. I admire your kindness, and I am very proud of all that you do. Thank you again for everything, my special man.
You make me very happy.

The End

Epilogue

Many of Saipan's factory owners (See Appendix) have moved their operations to countries like Vietnam and Mexico, where the costs of labor are lower, and the economic environment is more favorable and profitable.

As a result, Chun's story is likely being played out on every continent by women just like her—young girls in search of higher wages, new experiences, freedom, or a better life. The faces change, but the roles and experiences are the same.

As long as there is a quest for higher profits, a need for cheap labor in order to satisfy an insatiable demand for consumer goods, then the roar of planes carrying hopeful workers, the hum of the sewing machines, the din of voices on factory floors and inside barracks and cafeterias will continue. The triumph, the pain, the fear and hope and everything in between that you've experienced in *Chicken Feathers and Garlic Skin* does not end happily ever after when you turn the final page of this book. In the real lives lived by millions of real women every single day, the story continues....

*****

Order Chun's Interviews and Download MP3

Chun and co-author Walt Goodridge have been interviewed on radio on Saipan, on the Chinesepod Podcast during a visit to China, and by Mary Kay Magistrad for Public Radio International's "The World" during Mary Kay's visit to Saipan. This audio contains these interviews with Chun Yu Wang talking about her experiences as a garment factory worker on Saipan.

Write to Chun Yu Wang at

chunyu@saipanfactorygirl.com,

Chun Yu Wang
PO Box 503991
Saipan, MP 96950
www.SaipanFactoryGirl.com, where you'll also find a link to her Facebook Fan Page! Become a fan!

Find and order at https://www.waltgoodridge.com/store

Appendix ▲

The Rise and Fall
A 25-Year Timeline
Press Release
Ode to the Garment Factory
Garment Factory Closures & Dates
More Saipan Memoirs
Discover Saipan Series
About the Publisher

The Rise and Fall

The Garment Factory Era on Saipan has come to an end. From a high of thirty-six factories back in the mid 1990s, the last factory closed on January 15, 2009.

Gone are the throngs of Chinese girls walking arm in arm along Beach road. Gone are the vans shuttling them from their barracks to shop and congregate at Fiesta Mall, Sunleader Supermarket, San Jose Mart or 99 Cents Store. Sightings of girls riding their bicycles to and from work, holding umbrellas to shield themselves from the sun are few and far between.

What remains are opinions about the factories themselves, what they represented, and what their ultimate legacy will be in the ongoing story of Saipan.

There are those who saw them as a good thing, a boon to the local economy, providing jobs and tax revenue. Others see them as a blight, a blemish on the reputation and perception of Saipan, CNMI.

Factory Facts: 25-Year+ Timeline

Here are some of the facts of the rise and fall of the garment industry from 1983 - 2009 on the island of Saipan, CNMI, USA.

1983

☐ The first garment factory, Commonwealth Garment Factory, Inc. opens on Saipan on October 14, 1983.

☐ Quotas allowed for a maximum of 15,727 garment factory workers on the island of Saipan. Ninety percent of these are young women between the ages of 18 and 35.

☐ Garment factories help the CNMI economy by paying "user fees" and taxes.

☐ An economic study funded by the US Dept of the Interior's Office of Insular Affairs (OIA) revealed that with an average of $1,800 in income taxes per person, the apparel manufacturing industry, which currently employs about 15,000 foreign workers, contributes $27 million in income taxes alone to the CNMI.

☐ Aside from contributing to the public coffers through income taxes, each garment worker spends locally on consumer products. Based on foreign workers' average $50 weekly expenditure, all 15,000 garment workers cumulatively spend $750,000.

☐ CNMI used to have thirty-six garment factories, all located on Saipan. The garment industry used to contribute some $60 million in direct taxes a year to the local government.

1997

☐ Garment exports took a major leap in 1997, increasing by $235 million from $513.7 million in 1996 to $748.6 million.

1998

☐ The Saipan garment manufacturing industry exported close to $1 billion worth of apparel products to the United States in 1998.

Tribune: By end-1998, apparel exports from Saipan totaled $994.6 million, marking a $246 million increase from year-ago figures.

☐ In fiscal year 1998, user fee collection was about $37.8 million

1999

☐ *The Quarterly Economic Review* prepared by the Central Statistics Division of the Commerce Department noted that garment exports amounted $267.6 million in January-March 1999. The figure fell to $258 million the following period.

☐ At least 22 garment factories on Saipan were named defendants in the class action suit filed in the District Court here. It is the biggest court action facing the local garment industry. Among the companies named in the suits were The Gap, Cutter & Buck, Dayton Hudson, J. Crew Group, J.C. Penny, Sears Roebuck & Co., The Limited, Oshkosh B'Gosh, The Gymboree, the Associated Merchandising Corp., the May Company, Lane Bryant, Wal-Mart, Tommy Hilfiger, and the Warnaco Group. Major buyers of Saipan-made apparel products include the Gap, Liz Claiborne, Tommy Hilfiger and Ralph Lauren's Polo line.

☐ Total Garment factory sales peak at $1.05 Billion

☐ In fiscal year 1999, user fee collection was over $39.3 million

☐ *Friday, January 15, 1999 (Saipan Tribune)*
Lawsuit vs. garment firms alleges labor violations; Flor Pamintuan
  Twenty-three foreign garment workers yesterday filed a civil action in federal court against 22 local garment manufacturers alleging violations of federal and local labor laws.
  The plaintiffs brought the action on their own behalf and on behalf of a class of at least 25,000 similarly situated nonresident garment workers who are, or have been, employed by the garment manufacturers. Named as respondents are:

Advanced Textile Corp.,	Global Manufacturing Inc.,
American Investment Corp.,	Grace International Inc.,
American Pacific Textile Inc.,	Hansae (Saipan) Inc.,
Concorde Garment Manufac Corp.,	Joo Ang Apparel Inc., (Sam Kwang)
Diorva (Saipan) Ltd.,	L&T International Corp.,

Mariana Fashions Inc.,
Micronesian Garment Manufact Inc.,
Neo Fashion Inc.,
N.E.T. dba Suntex Manufact. Corp.,
Pang Jin Sang Sa Corp.,
Sako Corp.,

Top Fashion Corp.,
Trans-Asia Garment Forte Corp.,
United International Corp. and
US CNMI Development Inc.
Marianas Garment Manufacturing Inc.,
Michigan Inc.,

2000

☐ Feb 5, 2000: 25-year old Chun Yu Wang arrives on Saipan to work at Mirage as a sewing machine operator.

☐ Aug 6, 2000: Saipan Garment Factories Assoc (SGMA) suspends Eurotex, Inc. for "non-compliance with the SGMA Code of Conduct, substantial and persuasive evidence of a willful disregard of the code…"

☐ Oct 2000, garment factories start to close. (Eurotex Inc. was the first local factory to file for bankruptcy on October 21, 2000)

☐ In fiscal year 2000 (Oct 1, 1999 to Sept 30, 2000), user fee collection was over $30.4 million

2001

☐ The Zhida Market Savings Scam comes to light; Chinese couple ,Lin Zu Xiu and Li Rui Yuan convinced garment workers to deposit their money at Zhida Market in Garapan in return for a high interest after a month or two; Some factory girls lose in excess of $20,000 each in savings. Number of victims, approximately 45.

☐ Long City Traders Savings Scam; LCT is a jewelry shop that also offers financial services. Garment factory workers were misled into depositing their money with the company in exchange for higher interest rate. Number of victims: approximately 700. Owner, Kwan Yeun Cheung, fled to Hong Kong on Jan. 6, 2001. Media reports amount scammed exceeds $100,000, but many reject this figure.

☐ In fiscal year 2001, user fee collection was over $35.7 million

2002

☐ Total sales: $785 million

☐ In fiscal year 2002, user fee collection was over $30.4 million

2003

☐ In fiscal year 2003, user fee collection was over $29.46 million

2004

☐ Chun Yu Wang returns to China for first time in four years.

☐ In fiscal year 2004, user fee collection was about $30.1 million

2005

☐ Garment trade quotas end on January 1, 2005.

☐ Five factories close this year: Sako Corp, Neo Fashions, Express Manufacturing, Inc., Mariana Fashions, Inc., and Winners I.

☐ In fiscal year 2005, user fee collection was over $26 million

2006

☐ Six factories close this year: Concorde, Hyunjin Saipan, Inc., Am. Pacific Textile, Hansae Saipan, Handsome Saipan, & Poong In.

☐ As of Dec, 14, 2006, 21 garment factories remain on Saipan,

☐ In fiscal year 2006, user fee collection was about $19.5 million.

2007

☐ On Oct. 31, 2007 Jin Apparel Inc. filed a formal notice to Labor about its planned to suspend business operations from Dec. 31, 2007 until March 31, 2008.

☐ Sam Kwang, (where Chun Yu Wang has been employed since March 2005), files a closure notice; scheduled to cease operations in Jan 2008

☐ In fiscal year 2007, user fee collection was about $13 million

2008

☐ Sam Kwang closes a few days earlier than scheduled.

☐ Jan 8, 2008: Chun Yu sews her final garment at an illegal factory, walks away, and leaves factory life behind forever.

☐ User fees for the first 10 months of fiscal year 2008 totaled $4.79 million.

☐ Sept 28, 2008 - Saipan Garments Manufacturing Association officially dissolves

☐ October 31, 2008 – Garment Oversight Board (GOB) dissolves. 13,000 checks were mailed to members of the class action suit. 4,000 checks have not cleared. 1267 checks ($180,000) came back undeliverable. All the money from the class lawsuit settlement that garment workers fail to cash will go to a Garment Workers Trust Fund, according to GOB chairman Timothy Bellas.

☐ Chun Yu starts her new life as a waitress!

2009

☐ January 15, 2009: The last garment factory on Saipan closes.

☐ February, 2009: *Chicken Feathers and Garlic Skin: Diary of a Chinese Garment Factory Girl* by Chun Yu Wang is published.

FOR IMMEDIATE RELEASE:

The Last Garment Factory Closes on Saipan, CNMI
Closure marks end of controversial era on US commonwealth

Saipan, CNMI—Almost twenty-six years after the first one opened in October, 1983, the last garment factory on the US territory of Saipan closed its doors on January 15, 2009, ending a controversy-plagued era on this island in the Western Pacific.

Saipan was home to a once-thriving garment industry which, at its height, hosted thirty-six factories which employed over 15,000 contract workers (mostly women from China, and many from Thailand, Philippines and other Pacific Islands), generated (taxes) of $40 million/year for the CNMI government, and $994 million in annual exports to the world.

"It's a fascinating story, but much remains hidden about what things were really like here," says Walt Goodridge, business columnist for the Saipan Tribune, and "as told to" co-author and editor of *Chicken Feathers and Garlic Skin*, the only known first-hand account of the life of a Chinese garment factory worker on Saipan. "Opinions vary, but most workers felt it was a benefit to earn the money they did. This closure marks a significant turning point for the island's now primarily tourist-based economy," Goodridge added.

Saipan's unique relationship with the US allowed manufacturers to have "made in the USA" labels on garments sewn there, while benefiting from lower costs and a non-US regulated working wage paid to a mostly female, non-resident workforce. As the trade tariffs lifted, conditions became less profitable, and factories began leaving Saipan for other profit-friendly regions.

###

Ode to the Garment Factory

The last garment factory is closing
Bid the SEW-ers forever goodbye
And this chapter will end
and we'll turn a new bend
as the end of an era draws nigh

The last garment factory is closing
goes the bitter along with the sweet
Controversy and fraud?
Opportunity abroad?
Stories change with each person you meet

The last garment factory is closing
Some will say not a moment too soon
But from those who worked hard
daily seams and time cards
come the words of a whole different tune

The last garment factory is closing
ask the girls what they thought of it all
Most will say they were glad
for the chance that they had
and are sad that things slowed to a crawl

The last garment factory is closing
off to cheaper, more profit-filled climes
Shall we toast its demise?
Do we seek a reprise?
Or just strive now to make better times?

The last garment factory is closing
what on earth is our island to do?
Let our leaders contrive
a new plan to survive
so the nation can flourish anew!

The last garment factory is closing
let us hope now the future is kind
Let the Saipan of past
be re-shaped and recast
in an image that let's us all shine!

Garment Factory Closures (and dates)

1. Eurotex Inc. was the first local factory to shut down in 2000.

2. Global Manufacturing (2001/2006)

3. Trans-Asia Garment (2001/2006)

4. Concorde Garment Manufacturing Inc.,(2001/2006) (in 2001, Global Manufacturing and Trans-Asia merged with Concorde Garment Manufacturing Inc., only to shut down in 2006. (aka Concorde Garment Manufacturing/L&T International Corp.

5. NET Apparel dba Suntex Manufacturing Corp., merged with UIC, and Trans-America merged with Handsome Saipan Inc.

6. UIC (NET Apparel merged with UIC)

7. Trans-America merged with Handsome Saipan Inc.

8. Handsome Saipan, Inc /(Trans-America merged with Handsome Saipan Inc.)

9. Micronesian Garments Manufacturers Inc., (2002)

10. Diorva Saipan Ltd., (2002)

11. NET Corp. (2002)

12. Advance Textiles (In 2002, Micronesian Garments Manufacturers Inc., Diorva Saipan Ltd., NET Corp. and Advance Textiles closed down one after the other.)

13. La Mode Inc. filed for bankruptcy in 2004 changed name to Kyeung Seung Saipan, Inc.*****Kyeung Seung Saipan Inc. is formerly La Mode.

14. Express Manufacturing Inc., (2005)

15. Sako Corp., (name change to L&S 2005/closes Dec 31, 2007)

16. Marianas Fashions (merges 2005/closes 2008)
17. Winners II (2005)

18. Hyu jin Saipan (2006)

19. American Pacific Textile (2006) (In 2006 Hyunjin Saipan, and American Pacific Textile shut down their factories.

20. Grace International Inc., (April 7, 2007)

21. Top Fashion (July 2, 2007)

L&S Apparel Corp. formerly Sako, (Dec 2007)

22. Neo Fashion, Inc. (Jan 13, 2008; 88 alien, 13 residents)

23. Jin Apparel Inc., (Dec 31, 2007)

24. Sam Kwang (Jan 18, 2008; 157 alien, 14 residents)
(Sam Kwang is formerly Joo Ang Apparel)
Poong-In Saipan, Inc (Jan 28, 2008; 105 alien; 20 FSM)
(Poong In Saipan Inc. is formerly Marianas Fashion.)

25. Winners Corp (Feb 5, 2008; 337 alien, 28 residents)

26. Mirage (Saipan) Co, Ltd. (Feb 10, 2008)

27. Commonwealth Garment, Inc. (Feb 10, 2008)

28. MGM's factory (2008) was gutted by a fire a few months ago,
(sister company US-CNMI)

29. Onwell Garment Manufacturing have filed their notices of closure for Aug. 21, 2008

30. UIC shuts down (2008)

31. Marianas Garment Manufacturing
Kyungseung (Saipan) Inc (May 2008) (Kyeung Seung Saipan Inc. is formerly La Mode,)

32. United International Corp. ceased operations on Sept. 24, 2008

33. Michigan, Inc. closes

34. US-CNMI, closes 2008

35. Rifu Corp. ceased operations in December 2008

36. Uno Moda, the Last Garment Factory, closed January 15, 2009

Various Sources, including The Saipan Tribune & Marianas Variety newspapers on Saipan

More Saipan Memoirs ▲

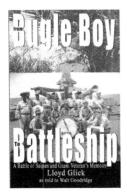

From Bugle Boy to Battle Ship by Lloyd Glick as told to Walt Goodridge

18-year old Lloyd Glick was watching a movie at a theater in Berkeley on Dec 7 1941, when they stopped the movie to announce Japan's bombing of Pearl Harbor. Four months later, with his parents' signed permission, he joined the United States Navy

From Bugle Boy to Battleship is Lloyd's fascinating account of his two years at sea aboard the USS North Carolina ship's band while it participated in the bombings of Saipan, Guam, Palau, Pohnpei, and battles in World War II's pivotal Pacific Campaign., as well as his hero's welcome return to visit the islands of Saipan and Guam 70 years later. *http://www.bugleboyglick.com*

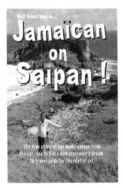

Jamaican on Saipan! The true story of one man's escape from the rat race to live a nomadpreneur's dream life..a travel guide for the rest of us!

"Once upon a time, there was a Jamaican civil engineer who hated his job, followed his passion, quit his civil engineering career, ran off to a tropical island in the Pacific, and started a tourism business so he could give tours of the island to pretty girls every day! This is his story." https://www.jamaicanonsaipan.com

Drinking Seawater
by Riza Ramos and Walt F.J. Goodridge

When Category-5, Super Typhoon Soudelor ravaged the island of Saipan in 2015. Riza Ramos, her husband and two children found themselves out in 150+-mph winds and flying debris seeking shelter after the roof of their home blew away. This is her story of before, during and after this harrowing experience.. Read more at www.rizaramosbooks.com

The Discover Saipan Series ▲

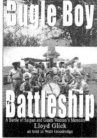

Saipan on Video ▲

Lieweila: A Micronesian Story: Narrated by Cinta Kaipat, a descendant of the first migrants, the film tells the history of the Refaluwasch people beginning with details of the early migrations and ending with their current presence on Saipan. *www.olomwaayband.com*

State of Liberty: Looking for America, is the pilot episode of a series which captures life, love and the pursuit of happiness here on Saipan. Filmmaker Dan Shor states: *"it's a story about the microcosm of the world that populates this tiny little island. Our lead characters are Japanese, Chinese, Chamorro, Carolinian, Bangladeshi, Filipino, Russian, and stateside Americans."* Everyone is represented, even the Jamaican(s) on the island. (No I wasn't in it, but much of the music in the soundtrack is the unmistakable drum & bass of Reggae!)

The Underwater World of Saipan is a 105-minute DVD showcasing the incredible beauty and bio-diversity of Saipan's underwater world. This DVD takes you on 7 distinctly different dives including The Grotto, Obyan, Banzai Cliff, Ice Cream, Managaha, Naftan Point and Lau Lau Bay. by Mike Tripp

Saipan Tour Apps ▲

Can't make it to Saipan? Take a self-guided, GPS-aided virtual tour of Saipan or Tinian (Rota soon!). A permanent record of over 200 waysides (info signs) and photos of popular tourist/cultural sites.

DISCOVER SAIPAN TOUR APP   DISCOVER TINIAN TOUR APP   DISCOVER ROTA TOUR APP

Preview at www.cnmitourism.com

Channels & Blogs ▲

"WWII tours, my daily life, special events, exploration by request & much more on Saipan, Tinian & Rota!"

Youtube: *@discoversaipan*
Blog: *www.discoversaipan.com/blog*

"My adventures throughout the Asia-Pacific region and beyond as a single, nomadic, minimalist, cheapskate!"

Youtube: *@jamaicaninchina*
Blog: *www.jamaicaninchina.com*

Saipan T-Shirts, Mugs & More ▲

Find them all at a store called W

Books, apps, audio, video, merchandise, courses, Walt's passion projects, freebies and more from a company called W!
www.waltgoodridge.com/store

About the Publisher and Co-Author ▲

 Walt F.J. Goodridge is from the Caribbean island of Jamaica and holds a Bachelor of Science in Civil Engineering from Columbia University. After seven years working as a civil engineer for the Port Authority of New York & New Jersey, this frustrated employee walked away from his career to pursue his passion for writing and helping others. His mission: *"I share what I know, so that others may grow!"*

In addition to identities as the "Hip Hop Entrepreneur author," "the Jamaican in China," and the "Ageless Adept," Walt is known as the "Passion Prophet," author of *Turn Your Passion Into Profit*, and his unique PassionProfit™ Philosophy & Formula.

Walt escaped from America to live on the Pacific island of Saipan, Commonwealth of the Northern Mariana Islands (CNMI), and has written several books about his new home: *Saipan Living, Doing Business on Saipan, Chicken Feathers & Garlic Skin, Saipan Now & There's Something About Saipan* and others.

He writes freelance articles for the *Saipan Tribune, Marianas Variety* and *Guam Business Journal;* conducts writer workshops to help aspiring authors; offers tours of the islands; has been featured in books and documentaries about the region; received a Senate Resolution for his contributions to CNMI society; and has received *three* Governor's Humanities Awards for (1) Preservation of CNMI History, (2) Research & Publications in the Humanities, and (3) Outstanding Humanities Teacher.

The Wall Street Journal, Entrepreneur Magazine, Source, Billboard, Time, Black Enterprise, Essence, Ebony, South Africa's *SArie Magazine* as well as "Guerrilla Marketing" guru Jay Conrad Levinson, and music industry pioneer Chuck D, and others have featured, quoted or endorsed his work. His books have been used as texts for university courses in the US and Europe. Walt currently owns and operates over 50 websites, has written well over two dozen books, 400+ business articles and over 500 "life rhymes."

He lives an untethered, minimalist, vegan, nomadic lifestyle, but responds to emails to walt@discoversaipan.com!

Download Walt's CV & Media Kit at
www.waltgoodridge.com

Made in the USA
Las Vegas, NV
14 April 2023

70587294R00108